Ancient Archives:
The SR Manuscript

Dear reader. This book is a manuscript of my research and writings on Semen Retention. I started making videos on Semen Retention a couple of years ago, and unexpectedly, the channel gained a loyal following of people interested in Semen Retention. Since then, many have asked for a physical copy of this work and this is what this manuscript has become. There are some edits and revisions - it is not word for word the same as my videos. Plus I have included supplementary writings from my SR course. If you are wanting to own a physical copy of my work then this book is for you! It is not an artfully designed story or a well organised encyclopedia. It is big blocks of information bound together into one manuscript on the subject of Semen Retention. I hope you find it to be useful.

Disclaimer: I am not a doctor nor a scientist. I am recounting ancient works and modern research and forming my own perspectives. I assume no responsibility or liability for any errors or omissions in the content of this book. The information contained here is provided on an "as is" basis, with no guarantees of completeness, accuracy, usefulness or timeliness. It is intended solely for the personal non-commercial use of the reader who accepts full responsibility for its use. Whilst I have taken every precaution to ensure that the content of this book is both current and accurate, errors can occur. The information presented should not be considered as professional, legal, medical or psychological advice. In all cases it is advised that you seek professional advice before embarking on any practices suggested here.

Semen Retention
The Death Of Your Old World

Semen retention will close many doors in your life.

People that you once got on well with will become antagonists on your journey. Numerous relationships that hinged on power will shift and become strained. Situations that you were previously experiencing will become no longer available to you. At times it will feel like the world is trying to step on your development, and perhaps even stamp out your existence. You are becoming a more powerful energy node, much like an electrical node, as a source of power for many others. The previously established nodes of power will feel threatened by your development, this is inevitable. The level of kickback you receive will be in direct proportion to your level of change and development. The only thing you won't be seen as on this journey is invisible. You will not have the pleasure of witnessing the intense effect you are having on the psyches of your friends and foes, but be aware that even without your active effort your influence is exerting an effect.

As the saying goes, when one door closes, another door opens. This is a particularly succinct analogy to people practicing semen retention. In the short term you will perhaps see strong opposition to your spiritual and physical development, but this is to be expected. Your power is increasing and this forces people to do the very thing they are most reluctant to do, to re-evaluate their previously held belief system. All of these held beliefs tie in to their sense of identity and where their own sense of being lies. It is a very dangerous game for people with issues of insecurity, to have to reevaluate where you and essentially they, fall on their own self imposed hierarchy, their hierarchy of human importance. When you force them to re-evaluate your social position it is like removing a block from a very fragile "jenga" tower that they have built up over their lives to deal with their feelings of low confidence and helplessness. This is not a criticism of people who have insecurities but rather a description of how those insecurities are commonly dealt with.

Start to see that these short-term perceived negatives are actually positives in the long term of your semen retention journey. How could they be anything else? As your value increases, more people will want to plug in to your power for their own benefits. You are a well of life and in a world where the top priority is survival, you represent the antithesis of death, and even just an association with you brings others closer to the source of life. You are the one in a million who has broken free from the slavery of sexual desire. It is difficult to articulate in words the intensely profound effect your abundant life essence has on people who come into contact with you, particularly people who are depleted in this resource.

Your accumulated energy is affecting the environment around you. Why do people, especially the elderly, have such feelings of delight and happiness when seeing a baby's face? Because babies are full of life force energy, they are the newly birthed seeds of life that will grow into fully developed human beings. They embody the very essence of life itself, and people who contain less of this essence, such as the elderly in general, will be all the more sensitive to its forces. We humans have an inherent attraction to life and an aversion to death. When we retain we are accumulating this same life force. Today's research journals will tell you the same, that the preservation of reproductive energies significantly extends life.

Please consider this point. That job you lost has put you back on the market with vastly more ability and value than you previously held and thus many more doors that were not previously accessible to you have suddenly become open. That relationship that is falling apart was only entered into on the basis of how your power related to theirs, whether that be slightly below, above or on an equal footing. Your massive energy increase and the development of your organism can easily upset the delicate social dynamic of friendship and business relationships. When an entity decides to depart from us on this journey, this is not a loss of connections at all, but rather it is life rearranging our circumstances and paving the way for our new being. With that in mind, accept the changes taking place and sincerely wave goodbye to your old world, as it fades away.

Like attracts like. This happens on the playground at school and it happens in adult life. This phenomenon is always going on around you, but at much subtler levels, and semen retention amplifies this process immensely. The universe, or perhaps this system we are inside of, is shedding our old connections and making way for new connections that will match the energy you are now generating. This process is encoded into the laws of nature. Into the algorithm.

If a zebra one day wakes up with yellow fur and starts developing big teeth and a lion's mane, for how long will his zebra friends and family maintain relations with him? Where will he fit in his current social group? He will be abandoned of course! How can the other zebras feel anything but threatened by this powerful transformation? As ludicrous as this scenario sounds, the social mechanisms at play here are identical. People act out of survival and self-preservation. Accept that your transformation is creating a new identity and a new reality for you that is undergoing construction - and that the building of new structures requires the destruction of old ones. Many people will have no place in your life as you evolve your being, this is a natural process, so embrace it, and be thankful that it will happen for you without your conscious effort.

If you pay less attention to the short term and more attention to the long term, you'll notice these patterns and be able to see them from a wider perspective. You may even reach the conclusion that every single perceived setback plants the seeds for much of the fortune that now exists in your current state of being.

You are changing. You are becoming an entity of powerful force. This process is not only about your internal transformation but the external transformation of your reality that is also occurring. You are being redirected to a higher plane of existence. Carry no doubt that these changes you are undergoing are for the ultimate betterment of your future and the world.

The Human Body

The human body is Mother Nature's magnum opus, a masterpiece of design with an infinite depth of intricacy that functions and navigates effectively on the physical plane of existence. Nothing in the human body developed randomly. Every detail of the body, from the largest organs down to the smallest cell serves its own very particular purpose.

Written in 1867 "Look at his form as he stands upright before you; how admirably it is arranged in all its parts ! The body is erect, yet the framework is so connected by joints and elastic tissues as to enable him to bend with ease and grace in whatever direction he may choose. His head, placed upon his shoulders as a cupola upon the structure, is so nicely adjusted as to be capable of being turned in almost every conceivable direction. The arms and hands are attached to the body by the best means, and in the best position to serve in ministering to his necessities and his pleasures. The legs and feet are so adroitly arranged as to balance the whole body in the most accurate manner, either in standing or walking, and admit of the greatest ease and freedom of motion, and speed of locomotion." (Miller, 1867, pg. 8)

This genial creation is the mark of genial design, a genial designer that possesses capabilities that far exceed our own human level of comprehension, or even level of existence. We humans may not have the capacity to truly understand the depths of such a design yet we have the capacity to recognise its intelligence, or rather the existence of such intelligence.

"Yet, wonderful and beautiful as are all these varied portions of man's body, the great masterpiece of workmanship is the human brain, with its hundreds of little counterparts in the nervous system. The brain with its continuation, the spinal cord, is the great centre, while the nerves are but so many minute telegraphic mediums of communication, penetrating the most distant and intricate portions of the whole body. The brain is the manufactory of thought, the home of the mind, and the medium through which we receive impressions of the material world." (Miller, 1867, pg. 11)

The mind is the true instrument of manifestation as it explores the abstract realms of the immaterial world and extracts these concepts into physical being. It is able to manifest and materialise almost anything from the dream world into physical reality. Within this masterpiece of work and from the very source of the mind, nervous system, blood and organs we carry the prized ingredient capable of recreating our very own being, the semen. Even at our current level of evolution humans are unable to recreate a fully fledged human being, without this invaluable ingredient. The sperm substance is of a "technology", for lack of a better word, far exceeding our own human grasp on creation. It is the epitome of the universe containing the properties of creation within itself.

The semen is absolutely sacred and indispensable to our very existence. It is the vessel that brought us to the physical plane, it is our very essence embodied in physical form.

One cannot state universally how best to spend our limited time on this physical plane, however, regardless of the endeavour one chooses to undertake, energy and vitality will be essential for the achievement of one's objectives. Higher levels of vitality in a majority of cases will equate to higher levels of progress and success. In order to achieve anything of note, one must pay particular attention to their limited energy supply and not waste their physical resources needlessly. The ultimate purpose of semen retention is the avoidance of unnecessary semen loss. Reproductive activity drains energy, induces old age and shortens life. This is a well-established concept in the field of biology, applied to almost all animals studied and is known as the Disposable Soma Theory of Aging.

A man's semen is certainly not a substance to be disregarded and expended for momentary pleasure. Every emission is a sacrifice of our own substance for the sake of creating a new being. This new being is the so-called "compensation" we receive for offering up a piece of our own life force. The laws of nature are immutable. Breaking these laws will inevitably come at a cost to our body, to our vitality, to our life. A fact perhaps unknown to many is that the violation of the nature's laws, in particular that of sexual indulgence will ultimately manifest itself physically and be recognised visually in the body and the face. People may not know exactly what you are thinking but will, in a deeply unconscious sense, recognise the *quality* of your thoughts. This is not a new idea at all.

"Your character is plainly written in your face. Beautiful thoughts light up the features. What you think has a whole lot to do with how you look. Your appearance has a great deal to do with your attractive power. The physical body is an external expression of the soul. You will find the person with well developed magnetic power, with a good face and a good physical body. Your thoughts and your motives mould your physical appearance.

As a man thinketh in his heart so is he. The man who lives a pure life will radiate the vibrations of purity and his thoughts will reach those with whom he comes in contact. You can tell a person of pure motives and high ideals by looking at his or her face, better than you can by listening to their words. Your disposition is written plainly on your countenance…It is not always the handsome person who is the most attractive. A person may have plain features, but by thinking beautiful thoughts he may become very good looking." (Dumont, 1914, pg. 54)

Be aware. You have been gifted the most valuable piece of machinery in the known universe. A human body. A human mind. It is a manifestation tool capable of fulfilling your wildest dreams. Look after it. Treat it as you would a valuable treasure. Give it rest, clean thoughts, exercise, fresh air, sun and good food. The good treatment of your body will manifest itself into health, looks, fortune and destiny. Treat these thoughts as sacred knowledge to be adhered to and respected. On this physical plane, your body is the kingdom of your soul. Treat it as such.

References

Abuses of the sex function, E.P. Miller, 1867, pg. 8, 11

The advanced course in personal magnetism, Theron Q. Dumont, 1914, pg. 54

The Art Of Life

Do you often think about your own existence?
Why you came here?
Where you came from?
Why you are existing as you, and not existing as somebody else?
Does it seem logical that you are in this body, but not in that body?
All the billions of bodies existing here, and you're in your one only.
You've perhaps even thought before, that this is just the luck of the
draw, that you have grown into your being by chance and that you had
no say in all of this; no hand in your own creation. That this was merely,
random.

As we observe matter and phenomena in the universe, the trees, the
insects, the flowers, everything, we find the highest levels of intelligence
and purposeful intent everywhere. A puppy grows into a dog and gives
birth to more puppies. Following a sequence of growth that ensures the
dog will follow the design of its own biology and not diverge from its
intended course, there is no chance of a puppy growing into a cat, for it
is destined to become a dog. This is written into its cells. It is coded in
the biology of every living thing. As a particular type of flower, for
example, will grow into that type of flower following a highly precise and
complex pattern of construction, development and growth. We have
mapped these consistently occurring patterns, or ratios of growth and
dubbed it the Fibonacci sequence. It can be found everywhere in
nature. The experience of this sequence resonates in our brains as
aesthetic beauty. The closer to this sequence, the higher the aesthetic,
and the higher pleasure we experience from its appearance, as it is a
visual representation of the universal design. Beauty represents the true
intended pattern of growth, the true nature of the universal code. In

essence, beauty represents truth. It is nature's intended expression. That's why we strive towards it. We are all seeking beauty, and we are all seeking truth. The closer we live in tune with nature, the closer to this ideal we become. Weston Price discovered this almost a century before with his studies of jaw malocclusion rates and facial development patterns in urban dwellers vs tribes people (Weston Price, Nutrition & Physical Degeneration, 1939) and concluded that the natural diets and natural lifestyles facilitated natural growth and thus more aesthetic development of the facial features.

The only way in which we can get closer to the attainment of this beauty, is through adherence to nature and all of nature's laws. Animals follow this law instinctively. All lifestyle habits that oppose natural law will carry the costs of deformity, degeneration and ultimately, unattractiveness. This is why semen retention brings us closer to the truth, to the source of life and its infinite power. As we learn to conserve our sexual power we learn to only use these vital resources when absolutely necessary, for the purposes of procreation. As seen with animals in the wild, copulation is reserved for procreation rather than for pleasure. The habit of constantly losing our sexual fluids via stimulation for purposes other than procreation, does not appear to be in line with nature.

Those on this journey who are seeking to align themselves to natural living will experience pain and struggle. The road to purify oneself from impurity does involve some pain. Quitting alcohol is painful. Quitting drugs is painful. Overcoming lust is painful.

The most negative aspect of semen retention is also the most powerful. Without the option of release you cannot escape your life. You must face it.

Ever since you began releasing your energies, you have been able to temporarily escape the pain of your existence and avoid facing your difficult life. You have had an escape door from rejection, from dissatisfaction, from loneliness, from sadness and from every other negative energy that infiltrates your being. The escape, however, was temporary and the use of this escape carried a greater cost.

Once you lock this door you are forced to come face to face with the pain of your own existence and your own demonic entities that inhabit your soul.
This is where your battle begins, learning to acclimatise to these dark energies.
Do not avoid a hard life.
A hard life can be a good life.
Be careful of associating an "easy life" with a "good life."
A good life is oftentimes hard.
An easy life is oftentimes unfulfilling.
Take the hard path.
It is there that you will seek fulfilment.
You must learn to overcome hard things.
Experience life's range of emotions.
Go through bouts of sadness and hardship.
Hardship means nothing.
It is your *response* to hardship that means everything.

Best to channel your energies into a craft or an activity.
If you don't know what to do, then start running. Go outside. Run to the shop. Run around the park. Tomorrow double it. Continue running everyday until you can complete a marathon. Then enter one.
Don't get caught up in deciding what you want to do. If you can't decide on anything, then just decide on anything. You can change the activity later, but take action now. If the day is not over, take physical action today. You are a physical being. Do not deny this part of your existence. Reading without movement, study without action, is not useful. If it's already night time, then schedule the action tomorrow. Do not meditate on it. Engage in the action with haste.
The exertion of your non-sexual faculties will be paramount during sexual conservation.
The brain and the testes are energetically in competition with each other in a fight for resources. With the conservation of your sexual

forces, you allow for surplus energy to all other aspects of your body. This energy must be used up!

"It is an admitted fact that as the mental faculties become more and more developed, the sex appetite grows constantly less; it is strongest among those of the lowest intelligence. As the lower passions become subdued, the forces formerly wasted are transformed into power, and not until then does man really begin to live. Life takes on a different aspect than ever before …your thoughts and aims are of a different nature. No longer content to live for yourself alone or to follow selfish aims, you become more altruistic and are ever ready to extend a helping hand to your fellow creatures. You become en rapport with your creator and seek to live in harmony with His laws; in fact, Regeneration means the awakening of the Higher Consciousness." (The Science Of Sex Regeneration, A. Gould & Franklin L. Dubois, 1911, p. 155)

You must learn something, and learn it well.
You have been asked to play with the cards you've been dealt.
Do not wish for better cards, but learn to play better.

Everyone has good cards and bad cards, you just can't see other's bad cards as easily as you can see your own. Don't let that stop you from feeling compassion for others. Everyone is in a constant battle for their lives. Everyone plays a character on stage but behind the scenes, behind their masks, they live a different life, of which you know little. The people around you are often more sensitive than you think. Your presence is affecting them a lot more than you may know. Do not be envious of other people's lives. They are battling demons that you are unaware of. Be thankful that at least your own demons are the ones you're familiar with. To know your own enemy allows you to prepare effectively.

Although you can't change the cards you can learn to use them to your advantage and play to your strengths. This is where your power lies. You are capable of so much work and so much change that is needed in this world. You are needed here, now. Entities come into existence on this plane because there is a necessity for their existence. There is nothing random about your existence. You are supposed to be here, reading this now. There is a reason these words found you. This information was meant for you because you're a seeker. And you're seeking truth.

The entire history of everything that has happened has resulted in you being placed right here, right now. This is exactly where you need to be. Your current position is as purposeful as the entire existence of this world and everything in it.

Do not run from hardship.
Do not run from grief
Do not run from death.
Death is necessary. Without it there could be no life.
Without up there is no down.
Without dark there is no light.
Everything in existence is made up of it's own opposite. The Law of Polarity. A central tenet of hermetic philosophy.

"Everything is dual; everything has poles; everything has its pair of opposites; like and unlike are the same; opposites are identical in nature but different in degree; extremes meet; all truths are but half-truths; all paradoxes may be reconciled." (The Kybalion, Three Initiates, 1908, pg. 32)

There was a time when you didn't exist. Now a time when you do exist. Then a time when you won't exist. And then a time when you will exist. This flux of the universe is merely a vibration, a wave of fluctuations passing in and out, up and down, back and forth. Each polarity allowing for the existence of its natural opposite. Let these waves wash over you without pushing or pulling, or holding on. Just let go. Everything is unfolding, in every way, exactly as it is meant to.

As Alan Watts said: "...regard yourself as a cloud, because of course, clouds never make mistakes. Have you ever seen a badly designed wave? No. They are always right. They always do the right thing, and as a matter of fact, so do we. We are natural beings, just like clouds and waves; however, we play complicated games that cause us to doubt ourselves. But if you will treat yourself as a cloud for a while, or a wave, you will realize that you can't make a mistake, whatever you do. Even if you do something that seems to be totally disastrous, somehow or other it will all come out in the wash. (A.Watts, 1998, pg.87)

With semen retention you are opening the door to your traumatic experiences in order to face your fears, your failures, your demons, and face them head on. This is the cure. Retention will give you insights into how to deal with pain. It will show you how to live with pain and become stronger. It is not that you should avoid pain. It is that you should become strong enough to be able to endure it.

Take on pain in a positive way. Accept your hardships as a challenge to rise up to and not be defeated by. They will bring you closer to nature, closer to beauty, closer to the truth of your existence. This attitude affects your visual image. It creates a quality of person that is to be reflected in the face and appearance.

"Thoughts crystallise into actual things. What we feel in our heart, harbour in our mind, think about, dream about, will in time develop from these tiny seeds into full growth. Hating someone will not develop your love qualities. A revenge seed cannot bring you anything but trouble. If we want to have friends we must be friendly. If we want love, we must have love. Whatever you send to another draws out of them the same kind of qualities. There is a law that regulates thought, which works out just as true as any other law. In India the developed yogis say, "If a man purposely does me wrong I will return him my ungrudging love. The more evil comes from him the more good shall go from me." The developed person of the coming day will understand how injurious are discordant thoughts, and will no more think of letting them into his mind than he would of taking some deadly poison. Your present character is the result of the life you have lived. An adept at character reading does not have to inquire of your past history to unmask your real traits.

He is able to read at a glance your thoughts and desires. When we see a face that is all tired and sour, you can tell the owner of the face never thought of beauty and joy, but instead lived a selfish and vicious life. When we see a face that shows a pleasant and agreeable disposition, we know that person has lived an unselfish, harmonious life." (Dumont, 1911 pg. 122)

The vitality of your stored sexual energies will grow inside you as that magic you feel when you meet a charming man, that same magic you experience upon seeing a beautiful woman, the same electricity in an inspirational leader of the people, the same magic in a musical composition that moves you deeply. They are all the same charge of electricity, all of the same nature. They all come from the same source, the source of life.

References

Weston Price, Nutrition & Physical Degeneration, 1939
The Science Of Sex Regeneration, A. Gould & Franklin L. Dubois, 1911, p. 155
Taoism Way Beyond Seeking, by Alan Watts, 1998, pg. 87
The Kybalion, Three Initiates, 1908, pg. 32
The Advanced Course In Personal Magnetism, Theron Q Dumont, 1911 pg. 122

Confidence

"If you hear a voice within you say 'you cannot paint,' then by all means paint, and that voice will be silenced."

- Vincent Van Gogh

Through saving money every day you accumulate fortune.

Through learning everyday you accumulate wisdom.

Through saving your sexual energies everyday you accumulate life.

What does it mean to be confident?

Why is confidence a trait more often associated with popularity, leadership and attractive people? Why is confidence less often found among people of lower social status and weaker body constitution?

We are taught not to judge a book a by its cover yet our biology betrays us as this is exactly how our minds have evolved to evaluate situations and people. This is an instinct that is hardwired into our brains.

Is it possible to become confident and attractive without the aid of our pre-destined genetics, upbringing and mental disposition?

In the retention community people often report that while on long-term retention they experience powerful levels of confidence, attractiveness and receptiveness from others. People experience greater ease in social interactions, stating that they find the right words to say at the right time and an increased ability to articulate their deepest thoughts with high precision. Others practicing retention claim to feel greater levels of motivation and self-assertiveness which can inspire the confidence to stand up to, and walk away from situations that are no longer benefitting them, such as jobs or relationships. How is it that the practice of semen retention causes such transformative changes within so many people?

Various literature has attributed semen retention to increased levels of neural activity, nerve and brain functioning. Many of those practicing retention are keenly aware of the physiological changes taking place within them. People experience a long list of changes both mentally, physically and spiritually, even within their first 30 days. Many become very aware that they are physically improving, that they are changing, and thus develop a conscious awareness of the inner transformation that is taking place.

Such an awareness of our own thoughts and thinking processes is known in the psychology sphere as meta-cognition, and developing this ability is said to aid in our mental development and learning processes.

This concept (without the label) had been recognised and expressed succinctly over 100 years ago. Written in the early 1900s:

"No one can impart power to you, because no one can create power, for all power comes from within. It does not take any more effort to be magnetic than not to be. To unfold latent power is very simple. When once you realize that you have power, you have confidence in your efforts, and this power irradiates your whole being. If the irradiation is weak, your power will be weak, but if the irradiation is strong, your power will be proportionately strong, and you may become invincible. We never know what we can do until we have something to spur us on to achievement." (T. Dumont, 1911 pg. 29)

It is this very awareness of our physical and mental improvements that gives us a new found sense of confidence and invincibility in ourselves. The physical structure of our own being plays an intrinsic role in how we view ourselves and the world around us.

On long term retention we experience a deep physiological transformation of our own organism. This not only encompasses the functional aspects of our body but also a marked increase in aesthetics, attractiveness and thus receptiveness from other people in social interactions. We are becoming a stronger concentration of pure energy and as time passes this concentration only increases.

A well-developed, sound confidence is an inevitable result of these improvements taking place from within the body, emanating in an increase in overall energy, vitality and health. An increase in electrical output power from the heart.

From the Hindu perspective comes an increase in Ojas, from the Taoists an increase in "jing essence", ultimately we are increasing the very essence of life itself from within us. Swami Sivananda, the Hindu spiritual teacher and Yoga guru, said that "semen retention nourishes the physical body, the heart and the intellect." (Sivananda, 1934, Chapter 6.)

How can we not exude more life force when this energy is being abundantly accumulated from within? This expression manifests itself outwardly as magnetism, charm, attractiveness and confidence.

Confidence from retention arises from an instinctual awareness of our physical and mental enhancement. We no longer feel the same heightened apprehension to perceived threats because we ourselves have become more formidable bodies of energy.

Our biological integrity is strengthening and we are becoming aware of it. Not only can we feel it within ourselves but others around us can feel it too, and on many occasions will make this fact known to us. Many of those practicing retention will begin to receive comments, compliments and new opportunities arising in their lives. It's as if a door to a new world opens up that we never previously knew existed. The transformation that occurs during this process is nothing short short of alchemic.

This is the practice of esoteric alchemy, the practice of transforming a substance of lesser value into greater value. Over time, day by day, the saving of our vital forces accumulates and goes to work to form nature's ideal form. All aspects of our development become geared towards the ideal form of human specimen that nature has intended. The closer we are to this ideal the more harmonious our existence becomes.

"By storing up sexual energy a man becomes stronger, healthier, and more vital. He becomes more ambitious too and creative in doing good. He becomes more patient and successful with people. And he develops stamina and endurance to see his works through to conclusions. So the sexually restrained male becomes more successful in general. Beyond that, he even develops occult power to influence things by sheer thought and will. In fact: To a Full Renunciant, God Gives All Power and All Worldly Authority. This is a Natural Law." (J. Lee, 1998, pg. 72)

People who receive much acknowledgement for their charm and attractiveness naturally become more confident in themselves. People who are recognised for their skills and contributions to a certain field become more confident in these abilities. People with a monopoly on money or social status operate from their own confident perspective. Of course there are many exceptions but in a general sense this is how confidence unfolds naturally throughout the physical world.

It could be said that all of these manifestations are indicative of the same thing. Energy. Attractiveness and robust physicality are a result of energy, whether that arises from the gift of genetic inheritance or from healthy lifestyle habits. Attractiveness is a result of uninterrupted natural

21

growth. This correct form of growth plays out across all forms in nature and is commonly referred to as the golden ratio of beauty.

People who were genetically blessed with attractive faces and physiques or even highly knowledgeable individuals within their fields tend to inevitably develop an inner awareness of their own powers through the feedback of those around them. People will let them know either directly or indirectly of their positively perceived traits and powers.

Confidence develops from an understating of this power that they themselves contain, a feeling of value created by an awareness of their own power in relation to others which can give them an overall sense of their place and influence in the world.

"No one will think more of you than you think of yourself. What you are is pictured in your appearance. If you think you are just ordinary you will appear just ordinary. The way you impress yourself is the way you will impress others. You can cultivate any qualities you desire and when you possess them you will express them in your face and manner. You have to feel grand to look your best. "Confidence is the very basis of all achievement. There is tremendous power in the conviction that we can do a thing." Without confidence there could be no miracles performed.

The Bible says: It was through the faith that Abraham, Moses and all the great characters were able to perform miracles, and do such marvellous things. All through the Bible the importance of faith is emphasized. "According to thy faith be it unto thee." Faith doubles our powers and multiplies our ability. Without it we can do little. By faith we can come in contact with the Infinite Power and learn the truth from the foundation source. It has always been the secret of great miracle-workers. Anything that shall increase your confidence in yourself will increase your magnetism." (T. Dumont, 1911, pg. 66)

Why does semen retention cause such a diverse cascade of benefits when practiced long term? Our entire filter through which we experience life is coloured by the abundance and quality of our life essence. When we preserve our essence over time and witness it building up, we sense ourselves becoming a much more powerful, energetic source in this world, a force to be reckoned with. We become a person that can work for longer, fight harder, influence further and out-perform all other competitors. With this knowledge at hand, when practiced consistently over time, we transform into a self-driven, motivated and energetic entity, capable of achieving anything in this world that we desire. As we become able to draw deeper on the universal source of energy, we realise that anything we so desire, is within reach.

References

The Advanced Course In Personal Magnetism, Theron Q Dumont, 1911 pg. 29, 66

Practice of Brahmacharya, Swami Sivananda, 1934, Chapter 6.

Julian Lee, Bliss Of The Celibate, 1998, pg. 72

The Gift Of Aggression

The state of aggression is commonly experienced during the time of semen retention. Why do so many experience this particular state when holding onto their life force?

The reason is, your vigour and vitality are increasing.

An increase in energy will reach all areas of the psyche. Larger quantities of life force will be distributed to each faculty of your brain. Your motivational power will increase dramatically as your enhanced synaptic connections fire more rapidly and function more efficiently to carry out mental to physical conversions. There is a line of communication between your mind and body that will function more fluidly when they are both in their most optimised and nutritive states.

The process of retention makes it easier for thoughts to be materialised physically. Any spark of inspiration will impel you to take physical action. This is why retainers are anything but lazy. The preservation of energy and increased nourishment of the organism makes it easier for one to convert thought energy into its physical equivalent. The body becomes more responsive to thought impulse and can swiftly carry out any intention originating from the mind.

This heightened awareness also applies to the state of anger. Your capability for aggression will increase. Perhaps this is why people become more assertive during longer streaks of retention. Their brain can no longer merely entertain dissatisfaction without physically acting upon it. We know that many people on retention leave jobs, leave relationships and make major shifts in their lifestyle during their streak. They are awakening a latent power that resides inside of them like a fireball of energy that transfers mental objects into the physical realm. This is the ingredient that impels one to take action, to physically respond to their own dissatisfaction and take the necessary steps to improve their life. Be grateful you have been given this gift of aggression. This is the catalyst of self transformation. You should understand that the universe is acting through you. It wants to evolve. You are the vessel to help it achieve this aim. As you stop the leak of sexual energy, your vessel can fill itself with the essence of the universe. The more this life force inside you grows, the stronger the evolutionary power of the universe will manifest itself into reality. With enough accumulation of this energy, your being becomes an unstoppable force.

As Mantak Chia said, "Sperm is the storehouse of male sexual energy. A single ejaculation has 200 to 500 million sperm cells, each a potential human being." (Mantak Chia, 1984, pg. XVII) The secretion of this fluid is what gives man his manliness, his characteristics, his physicality and his fighting spirit.

Written over a 100 years ago...

"It is easy to see the wonderful effect of these fluids in the youth and those that have lived continent lives have nothing but benefit to report from experiences. It is the secret of the wonderful transformation of the boy into a man. The powerful muscles, the vigour of nerve and brain, the manly form, the qualities of will, initiative and courage, idealism, the social instinct, sex love, etc., are all dependent for their normal development on the sex organs. It is a well known fact that through any cause the functions of the testes are destroyed before puberty, the essential characteristics of manhood take on a different form. They are likely to be completely without them, or only have them in a very minor form." (Gould & Dubois, 1911, Pg. 211)

Your aggression is a part of your masculinity. It is the yang energy that complements the yin, the feminine energy, that both exist within all of us. As a man you predominate the Yang yet allow the yin to keep the state of 'dynamic equilibrium.'

As long as the energy of aggression is used for a productive purpose you will go far. Through retention you are also learning the art of self control. Much like you control your lustful desires you must also control your aggression to prevent it from becoming destructive. On retention you become more assertive and thus it is easier to physically respond to a threat, even a minor one. What you are learning here is that the control of anger is much like the control of lust. Through retention you are learning not to act impulsively on thoughts and feelings and instead to harness those energies for a greater purpose, that of transmutation. You are learning the immense value of self discipline. Isn't it a coincidence that the habit of retention teaches you the very way in which to control the aggression that retention can manifest within you? You are being given both the symptom and the cure; the gift of aggression and at the same time the ability to control it. This is precisely what makes a retainer such a powerful entity.

'"Most powerful is he who has himself in his own power." - Seneca

Renowned Brahmachari, Swami Sivananda wrote on the topic of anger that "Anger and muscular energy can also be transmuted into Ojas. A man who has a great deal of Ojas in his brain can turn out immense mental work. He is very intelligent. He has lustrous eyes and a magnetic aura in his face. He can influence people by speaking a few words. A short speech of his produces a tremendous impression on the minds of the hearers. His speech is thrilling. He has an awe-inspiring personality." (Sivananda, 1934, Reprint 1997 pg. 51)

When you feel the anger flowing through you, remember, your strength lies in your ability not to react destructively with this emotion and to simply use the aggression to fuel your ambition and carry out your work. That is where its usefulness lies.

"To control aggression without inflicting injury is the Art of Peace." - Morihei Ueshiba

Channeling your aggression to productive work is controlling the fire. A controlled fire serves the controller. It will heat his house, keep his loved ones warm, light the lanterns to his village and if necessary, threaten total annihilation against his enemies. A wildfire out of control is of no use. A wildfire indiscriminately destroys everything in its path. That is why the fire must be harnessed, controlled and directed to be of any use. All on retention have this intense fire within. It grows and you must learn to handle its heat without it losing control. The loss of control can lead to destruction. Be wary of this. The successful control of this aggression will pay you large dividends. It will serve as the ultimate tool in your arsenal. Control is a reservoir of energy that you are free to draw from to protect your interests and further your objectives in life. Make efforts to embrace this masculine energy, to control it to the best of your ability, and in time you will become a powerful entity and a force to be reckoned with.

References

Taoist Secrets Of Love, Mantak Chia, 1984, pg. XVII

The Science Of Sex Regeneration by A.Gould & Dr. Franklin L Dubois, 1911, Pg. 211

Swami Sivananda, Practice of Brahmachrya, 1934, The Divine Life Society Reprint 1997, pg. 51

The Art Of Peace, M. Ueshiba, Translated by John Stevens, 1991, pg. 64

The Road of the Hermit

"Through the hostile landscapes
In the dead of the night
A lantern in one hand
guided by light
A staff in the other
He wanders the heights
In solitude seeking
The secrets of life."

To the retainer. You are leaving this world that you knew for so long. The ropes of desire that bound you for so many years, are now being cut away. Your vital essence is being restored. The essence that brought you to this realm, that has been absent for so many years is now beginning to grow and flourish again from within you.

This power will allow you to carry out your life's work. Day by day, as you retain it builds. As you receive nourishment from conserved energies, subtle shifts begin take place from within you. You may begin to see things differently, see people differently and feel things you've never felt. You may grow apart from the people in your life and feel the pull to retreat to a place of solitude. For a time you may even become the hermit.

Beginning the practice of semen retention is embarking on a journey. A physical journey will have you arrive at a physical location, but the process of self-transformation will have you arrive at a new state of existence. You are being a offered a transaction at no monetary cost. You trade in your worldly pleasures, and in return are transported into a higher state of being, a state closer to that of the gods. You become a powerful conduit, channeling the energy of the universe into physical forms.

For a retainer, the very essence of the universal life force will flow through your body and out your fingertips. It will be seen by others through your face, your aura, your words, your actions and through your creations. Others recognise this vital presence through all that is created under your hand. You are given the power to create masterpieces in any undertaking of your inclination. The divine touch of genius that coursed through the veins of Leonardo Da Vinci, Nikola Tesla, Isaac Newton, all celibates, is accessible to anyone with the ability to accumulate it. However, this is no easy feat. This act of conserving the vital forces requires the utmost discipline. The ability to resist the force of lustful desire is something very rarely seen in mankind nowadays.

When you commence semen retention you will delve into the depths of solitude. You will not be able to escape down the rabbit hole of fantasising and self-stimulation for temporary distraction and relief. You will come face to face with your own self and find deep, quiet, solitude. This is an acquired taste that may feel unbearable at first but with the accompaniment of time becomes the most exquisite flavour of all that life has to offer. Solitude becomes your medicine and will nurse you back to spiritual health. Others who are further along the path of retention may be well-acquainted with solitude and relish it. Semen retention will heighten the experience as you slowly unplug yourself from the draining pipes of your life force that have kept you distracted and idle for so long. A journey into solitude and spiritual enlightenment is symbolised by the hermit walking through the night. The retainer will inevitably find himself walking the path of the hermit.

Your essence acts as the light beacon held by the hermit, guiding you through the dark. You may be unable to see the destination yet this light is luminous enough to show you the next step to take. Solitude for many is a dark place. This is a journey of countless miles. You will walk a seemingly endless path up into the thick forests of the mountains, at times enduring snow storms, gale force winds and everything that mother nature has to throw at you. The hermit will remain on the path, undeterred from whatever comes his way, because the hermit knows this is merely a test. By starting this journey you boldly made the claim to nature of your intent to retain within you the essence of life, and nature is now testing that resolve of yours. It is one thing to claim renunciation, it is another thing to carry it out. But as you continue along the solitary path, you soon notice that things along the way begin to help you on your journey, things you initially saw as obstacles become your supporters, the environment around you is responding favourably to your pure thoughts, and as time progresses, the journey gets easier. The objects in your periphery, the characters, the landscape, appear to transform and change shape on this journey. But actually it is not the external that is changing, it is you. The subtler energies of the universe are becoming known to you, maybe for the first time. You are beginning to see deeper layers in the very core of existence. You are beginning to see what it is to be alive. The energies of people become visible to you, and your sensitivity so heightened that you can sense the intent of anyone that you cross paths with.

We will all be leaving this world on our own. Don't wait until that time comes to get comfortable with solitude. Solitude is a teacher and it will take you down to the depths of life. Do not avoid it. Pursue this loneliness and once you get a hold on it, embrace it. Learn it. It is best to see solitude as tranquil serenity. As you awaken, you channel God's wisdom, you learn much about the things that cannot be expressed with language. Throughout much of your journey you may not see the final destination you are traveling to, but a time will come when that destination makes itself known to you. Until that time, you will continue along the path, a solitary traveler, a hermit, with the knowledge that the vital forces will manifest themselves without your conscious action. All you need to do is create the conditions for its manifestation.

"I find it wholesome to be alone the greater part of the time. To be in company, even with the best, is soon wearisome and dissipating. I love to be alone. I never found the companion that was so companionable as solitude." (...)
"Silence is the universal refuge, the sequel to all dull discourses and all foolish acts, a balm to our every chagrin, as welcome after satiety as after disappointment; that background which the painter may not daub, be he master or bungler, and which, however awkward a figure we may have made in the foreground, remains ever our inviolable asylum, where no indignity can assail, no personality can disturb us."
(David Thoreau, 1849, Pg. 413)

Be solitary and content with your own company. Though you are alone you shall not be lonely. Spend time with yourself and the answers you seek will come. The seeds of originality and genius reside inside you but you need to still the mind long enough, until the waters settle and the ideas can spring forth. Solitude is the moment before creation. Coupled with the conservation of your life forces, your body and mental faculties strengthen immensely as you probe deeply the question of why you are here and begin to come to an ultimate realisation of your life's purpose, and an understanding of your own being. It is the catalyst that will inspire your most important actions on this earth. Allow yourself the time whilst retaining to really think about what it is you want, or even more importantly, how you can serve. This is the ultimate purpose of the hermit's journey.

References

'Self & Other' Audio Transcript, Alan Watts, n.d.
A Week On The Concord And Merrimack Rivers, Henry David Thoreau, 1849, Pg. 413

Semen Retention
Electric Fields

There is a vital source of energy permeating your very being.
It powers the processes and functions of your organism. An electrical energy charge that courses through your veins, through every cell of your body, breathing life into you. A battery. It powers the nervous system to send electrical signals through the body and to the brain allowing us to think and carry out physical movement and function. The strength of electrical charge is very much connected to your vitality and life force.

"…sexuality, if it be denied the reproductive expression, and provided that it also be kept from artificial excitation, seems to develop a sort of dynamic force or energy, which the nutritive, the motor, and the relational departments can use to their individual and collective advantage. On the other hand, those who unnaturally or excessively expend along sexual lines what may seem to them to be exclusively sexual energy, available only for sexual expression, thereby deprive the system at large of what might have become general stimulation and vitality. Indeed, the sexual department of a continent adult seems to be a sort of storage battery of vitality, a veritable reservoir for surplus energy. This energy, which seems so like a tremendous dynamic force, may be expended just as each individual shall elect: it may be wasted in lustful and abnormal sensuality; or it may be used partly for the legitimate purposes of reproduction, and the remainder in lustful practices; or it may be expended in exalting and intensifying the nutritive, the muscular, and the mental life. This remarkable fact is of great practical importance." (W.W Atkinson & Edward E.Beals, 1922, Pg. 79)

The retainment of sexual energy frees up available resources for all the other competing processes and functions occurring within the body. The more available bioenergy there is to utilise, the better the bodily systems can carry out those functions and processes resulting in less oxidative stress and higher maintenance of cell integrity.

"In the great battery of human life, man usually is the primary, or positive pole, woman the negative, or receptive: the one gives, the other receives; the connection of the one with the other opens a circuit through which the electric forces of the universe flow into both. But in order to construct a perfect battery, the natures of the husband and wife should be attuned to harmony; should be unweakened by abuses; in a word, each should be keyed to harmonious vibrations with the other. Where the conditions are such as these, a store of life energy is gathered in the body which throws out all worn out atoms; sends new life into those that are exhausted; revivifies the brain cells and thus provides a more efficient instrument for mental work, and generates a store of personal magnetism which inevitably draws to the individual the esteem of the people he deals with, as well as every good thing in the universe. This is the regenerative effect of the sex function, rightly, intelligently and purely exercised." (Gould & Dubois, 1911, Pg. 148)

"The elements in our bodies, like sodium, potassium, calcium, and magnesium, have a specific electrical charge. Almost all of our cells can use these charged elements, called ions, to generate electricity." (A.Plante, 2016)

These elements, along with more relating to bioelectric energy conduction are also found in the semen and prostate. One element of particular importance that is found in abundance in the semen and prostate is zinc. According to studies in the 1950s, the content level of zinc found in the human prostate gland was more than that contained in the liver, muscle, brain, testes or blood. (Mawson and Fischer 1951, 1952, 1953).

The body is powered by electricity. An electric field is endogenous when the electricity generated is not coming from an external source but is being generated internally from the firing of the cells. This electrical activity influences the behaviour of the surrounding network of cells.

"Essentially every organ and cell in our bodies uses electric voltage differences and ionic currents in the performance of critical daily functions. Every cell generates a voltage of roughly -70 mV across its outer membrane that is used for a variety of signalling and transport functions. For example, our retinal rod cells drive a relatively steady "dark current" into the outer segment and out of the inner segment (…) Even our cellular energy levels depend on voltage. All of our cells make their universal energy currency, ATP, in large part by generating a 200 mV potential difference across the mitochondrial inner membrane. With this abundant use of electrical signals in cellular and organ function, it should not be a surprise that endogenous electric fields are also important for normal development, regeneration and wound healing." (Richard Nuccitelli, February 2003, Radiation Protection Dosimetry 106(4):375- 83)

This electrical force that permeates the body has been written about in various contexts from modern to ancient texts spanning back thousands of years. It appears that many of the regenerative processes and functions that occur within the cell structures of the body are powered by these endogenous fields of electricity circulating within our organism. We are the walking storehouses of electrical energy, with regenerative abilities to keep us alive, and in this realm of existence. We may, as a human race, be powering something much bigger than us, something that lies beyond the limits of our own perception.

"Electrical activity has long been known to be important in sperm cells, and scientists had tried unsuccessfully to measure electrical currents in sperm since 1985." (Science Daily, 9 February 2006)

It has been established that in stallions, the available bio-electricity in the body, known as ATP, is required for the maintenance of membrane integrity in the spermatozoa. In simpler terms, bioelectric energy is required to keep and maintain the survival and integrity of the sperm. (M Plaza Davila et al. Reproduction. 2016 Dec.). It is reasonable to assume that similar such mechanisms would also apply to the human spermatozoa and that we would require electrical resources to create, power and maintain the sperm. Assuming this were true, then it would seem likely that the continual expulsion and necessary replacement of new stock may come at a biological price. The insufficient availability of this energy also known as ATP has been been known to cause oxidative stress via mitochondrial dysfunction. It seems, at least from my own perspective, that the constant loss of seminal fluids will require constant replenishment of said fluids and may not be conducive to optimal mitochondrial health. Furthermore, such a process could thus induce oxidative stress and accelerate the aging process prematurely. That the expenditure of life force comes at a cost to the organism should be of no surprise. It is an immutable law of nature and a widely recognised concept in biology.

"Since energy devoted to reproduction is not available for growth and maintenance, reproduction itself has a "cost" in terms of increased mortality or decreased growth of the adult organism. Thus, an individual that reproduces in a given year often has reduced survivorship and/or may reproduce at a lower rate in the near future. (...) Therefore, an organism may have greater evolutionary fitness over the long term if it postpones reproduction or limits the allocation of energy to current reproduction." (Ecology Center, para. 4, Accessed in Dec, 2022.).

The gift of life has afforded every living being a finite source of energy that can be used in any way they see fit. We can spend much of this energy on the activity of reproduction or we can invest it back into ourselves for the purposes of regeneration. The more bioenergy available, the more efficiently our cells can function and the less fatigue and oxidative stress we will experience in the long run. From nature's perspective it seems the purpose of our existence is for procreation, yet from an individual's perspective perhaps this isn't always the case. For many, health and longevity may be of a higher priority than procreation. There are no rules here, one must decide for themselves what values they seek to live by and how they wish to live. As we become attuned to our own source of energy we become capable of allocating that energy to the areas of our life that are important. This is why semen retention for many, is so important. It allows us to redirect these sexual energies and make them available to other parts of our body and life that require this energy for optimal function. It allows for greater maintenance, more regeneration and ultimately, more life.

References

Regenerative Power. By W.W Atkinson & Edward E.Beals, 1922, Pg. 79

The Science Of Sex Regeneration by A.Gould & Dr. Franklin L Dubois, 1911, Pg. 148

"*How The Human Body Uses Electricity*" Amber Plante
https://www.graduate.umaryland.edu/gsa/gazette/February-2016/How-the-human-body-uses-electricity/

(MAWSON CA, FISCHER MI. The occurrence of zinc in the human prostate gland. Can J Med Sci. 1952 Aug;30(4):336-9. doi: 10.1139/cjms52-043.
PMID: 14954495).

Nuccitelli, Richard. (2003). Endogenous electric fields in embryos during development, regeneration and wound healing. Radiation protection dosimetry. 106. 375-83. 10.1093/oxfordjournals.rpd.a006375.

Children's Hospital Boston. "Capturing the electrical activity of sperm: Experiments pin down target for a male contraceptive." ScienceDaily, 9 February 2006, Para. 13. <www.sciencedaily.com/releases/2006/02/060209164820.htm>.

Davila MP, Muñoz PM, Bolaños JM, Stout TA, Gadella BM, Tapia JA, da Silva CB, Ferrusola CO, Peña FJ. Mitochondrial ATP is required for the maintenance of membrane integrity in stallion spermatozoa, whereas motility requires both glycolysis and oxidative phosphorylation. Reproduction. 2016 Dec;152(6):683-694.

Cost of reproduction and allocation of energy" Ecology Center, para. 4, Accessed on Dec 10th, 2022, https://www.ecologycenter.us/population-growth/cost-of-reproduction-and-allocation-of-energy.html

Long Term Retention Is Rare
The Successful Retainer

"Mind: A beautiful servant, a dangerous master." - Osho

You must control your mind.

If you cannot gain control of your mind you will be unable to succeed on semen retention.

Very few people on this earth are on this journey. From that small number, an even smaller number are successfully retaining over the long term. To retain over six to twelve months is a rarity.

Your level of self-discipline is a direct reflection of your level of power.

Written in the 1930s: "Man is the first product of evolution to be capable of controlling evolutionary destiny. Endowed as he is with reasoning powers, he must independently decide upon his own behaviour, without the compelling guidance (of instinct.) Supplied with mind, he is expected to cooperate consciously with nature in her further evolutionary program. (...) Overstimulated by this unnaturally strong desire of his own making, man has looked for arbitrary ways in which to gratify it. Although reducing actual reproduction, he has discovered ways of unreproductive sexual action. But every such act, whatever form it takes, is a misuse of sex and uses up some of the life force that should be utilised for the support and the development of higher faculties. "The record of our race progress clearly shows how our upward movement has been checked ... by that misuse." (C. J. Van Vliet, 1939, pg. 17)

If your emotions override your actions, you will not be able to retain long-term. Think of the last time you were retaining and decided to relapse and end your streak for the sake of a few seconds.

This is where the battle is held. You couldn't handle the pressure and you gave in to your emotions. Emotions are dangerous. Respect their power and understand there is a constant war going on between your emotions and your rational mind.

Every time you submit to your desires and do something that you feel you shouldn't do, you are changing the course of your destiny towards the path of degeneration.

Every time you do what is right even if you don't feel like it, your mind is winning. Strength is winning and moving you onto the path of a prosperous future, your intended destiny.

Visualise these two entities fighting a holy war for control of your mind. Ultimately you get to decide which side will win.

Be aware that your mind wants what's best for you, but desire is willing to sacrifice everything for its own fulfillment. For it's own self gratification. Your mind is on your team. Sexual desire is a very powerful force that can be oftentimes dangerous. It is indeed helpful to see this desire as an external entity. A force that exists in this realm that can latch on to you and suck out your energy like a vampire, if you let it. This entity is very powerful and totally dominates the masses on this earth. To succeed on retention you must not submit to this powerful force. By not letting sexual desire feed on you, you are ridding it from this world.

Emotions are at times very helpful tools to have in our arsenal, yet they make terrible leaders. The leaders and successful people of this world have all had to fight this same internal war, and continue to do so with critical thinking at the forefront of their decision-making process.

The key to victory is simple.

Handle the pressure.

Embrace the sadness.

Wholeheartedly accept all of the negativity you are feeling and let it flow through you, knowing that eventually it will pass. Don't make any effort to relieve it, rather absorb it. Sit with it. Do not give it any influence over your physical actions.

Why are we so averse to sadness and suffering? Why do we not embrace hardship instead of going to great lengths to avoid it? There is much wisdom in sadness. Being sad gives us such a deep sense of appreciation for the good times, the good people, the good things in our life. Sadness is an essential component to living. Those that reject sadness and overreact because they're sad, those that can't handle this emotion will be forced to learn to carry it when it inevitably comes. If you wish to become strong and as a byproduct successful, then do not run away from sadness and hardship. Learn to endure it, and stick to your plan, regardless of whatever emotion you feel that day. This message isn't for everyone. But if you want to be in the top minority of successful people, then this is what you need to do.

Those who succeed are succeeding in handling pressure.

Even with the intense desire for pleasure they choose to look at the bigger picture, they understand the sacrifice they are making is for a much greater reward.

Even in their moments of weakness they don't act on this weakness. There is not even a chance of relapse because it is not something they can negotiate. Simply, they have resolved not to relapse and so they will not relapse.

It is ok to relapse. But be very clear on what you are not. You are not a successful retainer. You have failed. All the others who have continued past your date are mentally stronger than you are. By relapsing you have essentially drawn a line in the sand to measure your current level of power and self-control, and that line falls below every single retainer that has retained for longer than you.

This is important.

Don't give yourself a free pass.

Nobody who achieved retention long term, nobody who achieved greatness, gave themselves a free pass.

The secret to achieving this is...
There is no secret.
You just do it.
No excuses.
Nothing.

References

'The Coiled Serpent', Van Vliet, 1939, pg. 17

Semen Retention
The Power of Social Interaction

Many of our thoughts revolve around our social relationships with others. We spend much of our time unconsciously processing the data of our social interactions, forming mental webs of information regarding the people we interact with and gauging how those interactions affect us and our position in the social sphere.

For some, the negative words of others can leave us feeling down and dejected for days on end. Words tend to reveal deeper feelings and intentions that the speaker may have about us, and we may spend much time trying to decipher those words in order to reveal those intentions. The mind is constantly trying to establish where it is we stand in relation to everyone else. The mind exerts much energy analysing the daily words and actions of others, enabling us to make decisions regarding who are our allies, enemies and all gradients in between. This pattern of thought behaviour has evolved as a survival mechanism from tribal times when our survival depended heavily on our alliances with other people and tribes. Resources were commonly shared among alliances and thus networking was an integral part of survival.

The paradox here is that for many, our minds will go to great lengths to protect us from perceived social threats, but this stress will also take its toll on the body. Being in a constant state of over-analysis and worry can activate our fight or flight mode, and tax our body's energy reserves and nervous system, leaving us more stressed, nervous and ultimately prone to burn-out. Sometimes negativity may be directed at you by others via an overt verbal attack, via passive aggressive behaviour, or simply by the withdrawal of attention in order to elicit a negative response from you. It is perhaps best to think of social interactions as energy exchanges. Every time you interact with another person you are exchanging energy, and the outcome will be a more positive, negative or neutral state.

You will find that interacting with some people will amplify your energy whilst interacting with others will deplete you and leave you feeling drained. Why does this occur? Different chemicals when mixed together elicit different reactions. For example, when you mix cola and water there is no observable reaction, whereas when you mix cola and Mentos candy, the reaction is explosive.

Your human body emits it's own unique frequency of energy that is constantly expressing itself. We can become especially aware of our own energetic frequency when interacting with others as it serves as a reference point to ourself. When humans interact, their energies are also interacting and reacting to each other, much like the playing of two musical notes simultaneously that will result in either a harmonic paring or in a clash of dissonance. Like musical notes, human energies too will resonate with certain energies and clash with others.

If our energies are vibrating at a frequency similar or on the same scale as another they harmonise and are felt by both entities positively as they form a synergistic bond.

This is the feeling you get when you have a great interaction with someone who seems to be on the same wavelength as you. You can feel your interacting energies harmonising with each other and feeding you positive vibrations.

When you find it difficult to get along with someone it is perhaps not "your fault" or "their fault" so much as it is a dissonance of your energies. Conceivably there is nothing personal here. It is not water's fault that it cannot mix with oil, just as it is not oil's fault that it cannot mix with water. The substances are not structured to merge. There is no reason for you take any such negative social interaction to heart.

Many have reported that on their semen retention streaks they experience uncontrollable emotions and stronger irritability in social situations. Situations that were not so stressful in the past may become harder to deal with whilst retaining. Other's behaviour may suddenly be felt as highly provocative and our reactions can be surprisingly strong. At times we may even experience outbursts of anger.

Now that you have stopped the constant drain on your energetic resources via semen loss, your brain has more energy at its disposal and many areas of brain activity may become hyperactive. Emotions are perceived more strongly, our gut reactions can become almost palpable and impulses to assert ourselves more aggressively may manifest. The increase in testosterone (as evidenced in studies and often anecdotally reported) may also play a role in increased aggressiveness. It will take some getting used to this new state of being and learning how to deal with this excess energy. On a physical level, those practicing retention would greatly benefit by working their bodies physically to the point of fatigue each and every day. Engaging the body in much work and physical activity (as well as mental activity) so that by the end of the day we feel a strong desire to rest, is optimal.

In dealing with these physiological changes during retention it would help to remember the following:

We have no control over the output of others yet we have total control over how we react. An insult is not an insult, until we decide it to be.

To not allow the words of others to negatively affect our emotions is one of the most important rules we can learn to improve our happiness and ultimately our health.
Commencing semen retention involves restricting your body from experiencing orgasm. An orgasm is much like any other drug as it causes significant amounts of dopamine to be released into the system,

creating a temporary relief and numbness from stress. You have become used to this instant reward. This is perhaps why people especially tend to relapse when under stress or experiencing loneliness. Much like a drug, it can take the edge off life. People easily become addicted to this feeling and giving up this luxury can sometimes be a lot harder than one first envisages. There is an adjustment phase where you will have to get comfortable with being uncomfortable. For many, this is where relapse begins. Your own resolve is tested. We get to decide whether or not to be offended by other's actions.

To not allow the words of others to have an emotional impact on us is a skill that can be soundly developed. It is a central principle of stoic philosophy and will help you deal with people and life in general but especially on your retention journey. You may have learnt this in the playground: "Sticks and stones may break my bones but names will never hurt me."

Often though, it is not an outright "attack" that we must face but perceived passive aggression such as being ignored or socially excluded. These more covert methods of social interaction are more commonly applied in modern society because an outright physical attack would bring unwanted attention and culpability, whereas a passive attack allows for plausible deniability.

For many reading this, their automatic response to insult is offence and a feeling of being personally targeted. Feelings of worthlessness or of not being a "valid human being" or member of the social group can also be common.

The way to deal with such a situation is to not take it as an insult. It is only an insult because you perceived it to be. You could have perceived the words in any way you wished and you decided to perceive them in a highly personalised way, perhaps even connecting many of your self-perceived shortcomings to the negative words of your companion. You can change your perception of an insult and the effect will dramatically improve your mental well being.

"It is in our power to have no opinion about a thing, and not to be disturbed in our soul; for things themselves have no natural power to form our judgements." (Marcus Aurelius, trans. G. Long, 6.52, 1862)

There are many on this earth who do not feel the slightest bother by the words of others. They are nothing more than whispers in the wind. They realise that the people they are interacting with live in totally different realities and their perspective holds no bearing on their own existence.

Remember you and your fellow man do not inhabit the same brain, you do not inhabit the same universe, just similar versions. You are playing two very different versions of a game or watching the same movie but each from a different character's perspective. Sometimes we get to see the antagonist's perspective in later movie sequels and realise they weren't so bad all along. A good example of this is from the recent re-make of the movie "The Karate Kid" where we see the story from the bad guy's perspective and thus sympathise with his journey much more so than we did so in the original film. Perspective is everything.

Even the way we perceive colours may vary from human to human. How are you so sure that the the light blue you are looking at is not a darker shade or different colour in the eyes of your companion? It is difficult to confirm that the blue I'm looking at is the exact same version of blue that you are seeing.

This is an important point to keep in mind when experiencing conflict and a difference of opinion with others. We need to understand that they don't see things in exactly the way we do because they are in a different version of this world than us. They are playing a different game. This knowledge should free you. No one person's opinion has anything to do with you. Their opinion is just their reaction to a version of you in their story and that is not the real you at all! That version they are hating on is not you, it is a character that exists in a different universe from where you exist. It is a shadow of a shadow. There is nothing to be taken to heart about this as it has nothing to do with you.

The person you interact with lives in a universe where they are the hero and are trying live happily ever after, and anything that appears to hinder this objective gets violently rejected.

Try to develop a sense of sympathy for this perceived enemy. Next time you're insulted by another person, keep in mind: "Every man has his secret sorrows which the world knows not; and often times we call a man cold when he is only sad." (Henry Wadsworth Longfellow, Bk. III, Ch. IV, 1839).

When you experience someone being undeservedly antagonistic towards you, realise they are merely fighting with themselves. Those words hold no bearing upon you and your existence. When you experience someone wilfully ignoring your existence, remember the reflection they see of you is reflecting something in themselves. Developing a sense of compassion is perhaps more useful than anything else. People don't set out to be evil, they think they are doing the right thing, yet many are still operating from lower levels of consciousness, or lower emotional states with lower energy frequencies. Be thankful you have elevated your own awareness enough to be able to see this and don't allow them to pull you down to their level of thinking. Develop compassion.

References

Meditations, Marcus Aurelius, trans. G. Long, 6.52, 1862

Hyperion, Henry Wadsworth Longfellow, Bk. III, Ch. IV, 1839

Recovery From Semen Loss

Is a full of recovery of years of ejaculation possible?

Can you return your organism back to it's optimal state, back to the state of an organism that had never released in the first place? Can we reverse years of semen loss?

Perhaps the following proverb is appropriate here..

"The best time to plant a tree was 20 years ago. The second best time is now."

Provided you are not on your death-bed, moments away from expiration, then recovery should be very possible. The rate and level of your recovery will depend on the natural constitution of your body and the level of action you're willing to take to cultivate healthy habits. The loss of your vitality is essentially what you are trying to remedy. Just as the depletion of your physical forces occurred gradually over many years, so will your recovery process take years to correct. The good news is you can start to notice the smaller benefits almost immediately upon commencement of retention.

Said in 1900: "Let us emphasise at the very start that no drugs, no tonics of any kind (...), can be of the slightest influence towards creating or strengthening sexual power. The remedy must come from within, must accompany the building-up of all the physical forces. The circulation of the entire body must be awakened and brought up to a normal standard by natural means. Nature! Depend on Nature and natural means entirely if you desire a cure. There is no excuse for impotence. One should retain the power of sex all through life, and if the laws of Nature have not been grossly violated, this can be done in every instance. If your powers in this way have been depleted or destroyed, rejuvenate them again by building up the nervous and physical forces.' (MacFadden, 1900, pg. 115)

The built up vitality in our body, known in Brahmachrya as the Ojas, is present in every cell, like a form of electricity that energises the structure. The stimulation of the prostate draws on this vital energy and converts it to its physical manifestation, semen.

The creation of this precious fluid starts at the sexual thought impulse, and is achieved by drawing energy out of the brain, nervous tissues and cells of your body and using that energy to produce semen in the testes. This diverts valuable energy away from the organs and tissues. This is perhaps why many doctors of note throughout history attributed nervous debilitation and insanity to excessive masturbation. Think about it. The ingredient to create such an energetic life-giving fluid is none other than your own life essence. We have been built to be able to make this sacrifice of our energy for the sake of the creation of a new human being. But if we are not using it for the purpose of procreation then ultimately what are we gaining from this sacrifice? We are paying a huge cost for momentary pleasure, by giving up a small portion of our own life force. It was said long ago "It takes flesh, to make flesh."

"One of the students of Dhanvantari approached his teacher after finishing his full course of Ayurveda and asked him: "O Bhagavan, kindly let me know the secret of health now." Dhanvantari replied: "This Veerya (seminal energy) is verily Atman. The secret of health lies in preservation of this vital force. He who wastes this energy cannot have physical, mental, moral and spiritual development."
If the Veerya is lost, Prana gets unsteady. Prana is agitated. The man becomes nervous. Then the mind also cannot work properly. The man becomes fickle-minded. There is mental weakness."

(Sivananda, n.d.-b)

For recovery on semen retention you will need the following:

Time. Much time.

If this habit has been indulged for over a decade then perhaps realise your recovery will take numerous years of concentrated effort. That regeneration and recovery is even possible should motivate you regardless of the time required. Even in the first six to twelve months of complete retention you will experience life-changing results, but this is perhaps only the tip of the iceberg. Understand that retention is no quick fix. This habit of conservation if practiced long enough may enable recovery of your faculties to their optimal state, and fill your organism with untold levels of energy that will permeate through every fibre of your being.

Exercise. You will need to move your body and work up a sweat at least a twice a day. As MacFadden wrote: "Muscular exercise, adapted to the needs of the individual, tends to produce, in every case, a more normal condition. For instance, if one is too fleshy to be in normal health, it will take off flesh; if too thin, it will add flesh. This ability of physical culture to bring about the highest degree of normal health is exemplified with equal emphasis in sexual life. Those who suffer from weakness in this way will find in specially adapted training the only safe means of cure. As the muscles develop, the digestive power increases, the circulation improves, the nerves are strengthened, and the mind refreshed with renewed confidence. This building up of the physical strength affects beneficially every organ of the body. The same can be said of its effects on those suffering sexually from an excess of animal life. This is a disease just the same as the other extreme, and this surplus energy can be absorbed and used to advantage if expended in muscular exercise. Not only does the muscle and nerve power increase, and the general health vastly improve when this method is followed, but the unusual and unnatural strength of this abnormal desire disappears, creating in reality a greater, safer strength, and removing the feverishness of an over-wrought nervousness.'

"The effect of cultivating sexual vigour by building up the muscular and vital powers of the body cannot be fittingly described. If all powers in this way are lost, or if they seem to have so diminished in vigour that the intense desire of vigorous pulsating youth has disappeared, they can be entirely regained by natural processes assisted by the muscular movements described here; of rich blood in copious quantities to every part of the body which results from these exercises is one of the salient features necessary in order to regain the sexual powers. Under the influence of proper exercise for every muscle of the body, the heart, with quick and strong and greatly accelerated pulsations, forces the blood with increased power through the arteries and capillaries, drives the impurities out through the great purifying organs, the skin and kidneys, and causes every organ of the body to be rejuvenated and strengthened." (MacFadden, 1900)

Sleep: To reap the restorative benefits of sleep, follow this simple rule. Sun up, be up, sun down, lay down. The closer you adhere to this schedule, the closer your restorative benefits will be. This is how your circadian rhythm is programmed and thus how your body can fully make use of sleep. If you sleep early for consecutive days your body should develop a natural waking up time roughly 6-8 hours after sleep. Try to allow yourself to awaken naturally and set an alarm at the latest possible time just in case, for whatever reason your body misses this time. For the most part your body will begin to set it's own alarm clock and this is the most natural time to rise. If you find you are waking in the middle of the night, you are perhaps not expending enough physical and/or mental energy before sleep and should engage in some activity that will work the body and mind to fatigue. Two good recommendations for both mental and physical exercise are outdoor running and chess.

Foods: Nowadays there are countless perspectives on the most appropriate diet for the body. Each come with pros and cons. In terms of regeneration, the best foods are of high (unprocessed) quality, rich in minerals and easily digestible. Rice, meats, vegetables and soups. Depending on one's body weight, the calorie intake may be adjusted accordingly. Obviously, underweight people need more calories and those who are overweight need less. Vices: The renunciation of all unhealthy vices such as cigarettes, drugs and alcohol.

Following a lifestyle of good foods, outdoor exercise and sleep will greatly aid you on your journey of semen retention. All such practices will contribute towards revitalising energy stores, organ regeneration, blood quality improvement and an overall improvement of the structure of your organism and subsequently its appearance. Keep these realisations in mind and your long-term goals for recovery will gradually materialise. With consistency you will inevitably experience a restorative transformation back to your optimal level of physical health.

References

The Virile Vowers of Superb Manhood, B. Macfadden, 1900, pg. 115

Practice of Brahmacharya, Swami Sivananda, (n.d.). https://www.sivanandaonline.org/?cmd=displaysection§ion_id=1214

Physical Beauty

Why are we attracted to beauty?

It's a signal.

A signal of optimal immunity and health. Then why are we are attracted to good health?

Survival. We survive with good health and immunity. We die from ill-health and physical degeneration. Beauty and good health are the antithesis to death and physical degeneration. We gravitate towards anything close to the source of life, and beauty is a symbol of life.

When our organism exists in an optimal growth state, it will develop in accordance with nature's design. Templates of design exist within nature and many say that they indicate a designer. One such design is known as the Fibonacci sequence. There is much to these designs that we are yet to fully comprehend, however, when allowed to grow in accordance with nature, we seem to adhere to some preordained template of growth. We can instinctively sense this pattern of growth through the aesthetics of beauty. Beauty is a signal to us that nature is taking her course, uninterrupted, and as intended.

Each human body in existence today is the result of many human lives before us that reproduced and died over and over to create the body we have today. The lifestyles of our ancestors also played a role in our current physical condition. Whilst we have no control over our ancestral inheritances, we do have agency over our current life. If we choose to live in accordance with the laws of nature we will grow and develop towards nature's ideal sequence and thus towards beauty itself. The ejaculation and subsequent loss of seminal fluids is a highly taxing process on the human organism, to the extent that repeated expenditure of semen will markedly decrease the lifespan of the organism. Semen contains highly nutritious fats, lipids, minerals, phosphorus and other essential minerals found throughout the body and in particular, concentrated amounts within the brain and nervous tissues. Expending these elements on a regular basis leads to deficiency and degeneration.

If we wish to strive for beauty we must first rid ourselves of the habits that prevent optimal conditions for the organism. Sexual excess is the first habit we must address. If you have kept this habit for many years, do not expect change to occur immediately. It is a long term process. It took many years to reach your current state and it will take a significant amount of time to restore optimal growth and development. If you're reading this and wanting to increase your health, beauty and overall integrity, then the time is now. Put a stop to your semen loss.

Semen & Ojas
The Elixir of Life

What is Ojas?

Ojas is a Sanskrit term that loosely translates to vigour, life force, health and spiritual growth. According to Ayurvedic philosophy It is a sacred substance that can be built up in the body through the long-term preservation of sexual energy.

Swami Vivekananda said: "The Ojas is that which makes the difference between man and man. The man who has much Ojas is the leader of men. It gives a tremendous power of attraction. Ojas is manufactured from the nerve – currents. It has this peculiarity: it is most easily made from that force which manifests itself in the sexual powers. If the powers of the sexual centres are not frittered away and their energies wasted, they can be manufactured into Ojas." (Vivekananda, 1913, Volume VI)

Ojas is considered to be the nectar or life. Sexual energy creates the most valuable substance in our existence. Semen. The value and importance of this substance cannot be overstated. It is the seed of existence, perhaps the seed of the universe. Holding on to this precious fluid will increase and intensify the universal forces from within us.

In 1943 Swami Jagadiswarananda wrote:

"Retention of Semen creates the eight Dhatu called Ojas' in our body. Ojas is what is called by the westerners as 'magnetism.' Ojas is the spiritual force...." (Jagadiswarananda, 1943, p. 43)

Throughout many cultures over history, the preservation of the seed has been strongly encouraged. According to Ayurveda, the concept of Ojas exists in which the preservation of semen builds up this powerful substance that rejuvenates the mind, body and spirit. It is said to provide the being with immense physical and mental vitality and vigour. It is a quality that is found in abundance among healthy individuals. In Ayurveda a lack of Ojas is blamed for many cases of physical and mental degenerative illness.

On the subject of Ojas, Swami Vivekananda also went on to say that: "It is only the chaste man or woman who can make the Ojas rise and store it in the brain; that is why chastity has always been considered the highest virtue. A man feels that if he is unchaste, spirituality goes away, he loses mental vigour and moral stamina. That is why in all the religious orders in the world which have produced spiritual giants you will always find absolute chastity insisted upon." (Vivekananda, 1896, pg. 52)

Taoist Master Mantak Chia gives his perspective on semen preservation, stating: "Extraordinary powers, including healing and clairvoyant perception, may evolve when one retains the semen and drives its power back up into the body. Many gifted minds have held that if one could retain these fluids for one's entire life, the body would not decay after death. The Saints—Christian, Buddhist, Moslem, or Taoist—all used the power dwelling in the vital seed to perform 'miracles.'"

If you wish to tap into the deepest state of consciousness and manifest creative genius, then you must preserve your seed. And over time you will accumulate this sacred elixir within you. You will develop abilities and take action far beyond your wildest imagination.

References

Complete Works, Swami Vivekananda, Lessons on Raja Yoga, 1913, Volume VI,

Taoist Secrets Of Love, Mantak Chia, 1984, pg. 3

Continence & Its Creative Power, Swami Jagadiswarananda, 1943, pg. 43

Raja Yoga, , Vivekananda, 1896, pg. 52

Deep Quotes on Semen Retention

"The sexual glands are all the time secreting the semen. This secretion should be utilised for enhancing one's mental, physical and spiritual energy. He, who would learn to utilise it thus, will find that he requires very little food to keep his body in a fit condition. And yet he will be as capable as any of undertaking physical labour. Mental exertion will not tire him easily nor will he show the ordinary signs of old age. Just as a ripe fruit or old leaves falls off naturally, so will such a brahmachari when his times comes pass away with all his faculties intact." (M.Gandhi, 1954, pg. 26).

"It is a medical and physiological fact that the best blood in the body goes to form the elements of reproduction in both the sexes. In a pure and orderly life, this matter is reabsorbed. It goes back into circulation ready to form the finest brain, nerve and muscular tissues. This vital fluid of man carried back and diffused through his system makes him manly, strong, brave and heroic. If wasted, it leaves him effeminate, weak and physically debilitated and prone to sexual irritation and disordered function, a wretched nervous system, epilepsy, and various other diseases and death. The suspension of the use of the generative organs is attended with a notable increase of bodily and mental and spiritual vigour." (Dr Nicholas as cited by Atkinson, 1922).

"In view of the richness of the semen in lecithin, cholesterol, phosphorus and other constituents of nervous and brain tissue it is clear that it is incontinence, or loss of these valuable nerve-nourishing substances which, by promoting undernutrition, is responsible for disturbed functioning of the nervous system and brain."
(R. W. Bernard, 1957, pg. 1)

"If a man has an emission of semen, he shall bathe his whole body in water and be unclean until the evening. And every garment and every skin on which the semen comes shall be washed with water and be unclean until the evening. If a man lies with a woman and has an emission of semen, both of them shall bathe themselves in water and be unclean until the evening."
(The Bible, Leviticus 15:16-18 The Message (MSG))

"All waste of spermatic secretions, whether voluntary or involuntary, is a direct waste of the life force. It is almost universally conceded that the choicest element of the blood enters into the composition of the spermatic secretion. If these conclusions are correct, then it follows that a chaste life is essential to man's well-being." (Dr. EP Miller, n.d).

References

Key To Health, M.Gandhi, 1954, pg. 26

Dr.Nicholas (as cited in Regenerative Power, Atkinson, 1922, pg. 67)

Science discovers the physiological value of continence, R. W. Bernard, 1957, pg. 1

The Bible, Leviticus 15:16-18 The Message (MSG)

Dr. EP Miller, original source unknown, (n.d.).

Sperm Quality - Intelligence Research Findings

It has been said by various authors that many of the great minds in human history practiced celibacy. From Isaac Newton to Nikola Tesla, many of the ancient Greek philosophers, modern philosophers, artists and so on..

Upon hearing of this information, I researched many study journals on the topic of semen and came across one that uncovers the connection between semen quality and 'genius.'

In 2009 a research journal was published that studied the relationship between semen quality and human intelligence. The results were very interesting. They discovered a positive correlation between one's sperm quality and intelligence. (Pierce. A, et al., 2009)

Three semen measures were analysed in the study: sperm concentration, sperm count and sperm motility. These three aspects were selected as they are all associated with fertility. To determine intelligence levels, five neuropsychological tests that the participants had undertaken were analysed.

Conclusions found that intelligence correlated significantly and positivity with all three measures of semen quality.

In short, from this study we may perhaps infer that higher sperm quality has a positive correlation to higher intelligence.

This notion that semen preservation nourishes the brain and that semen loss leads to brain degeneration has been shared throughout the ages in literature, from medical doctors to religious leaders to swamis and so on. This study can give us further insight into how intelligence and our brain are intrinsically connected to the integrity of our semen and prostate. This brain/semen link has been discussed extensively by R. Bernard in his writings over 60 years ago in which he finds the content of both the brain and semen to rich in lecithin.

"The grey matter of the brain contains 17% lecithin, which is the essential and indispensable medium through which the higher intellectual processes manifest themselves. The greater the purity in which lecithin is found, the higher the intelligence of the animal, even in insects." (Bernard, 1957, pg. 33)

Could sexual abstinence be the key to generating the health of your brain and unlocking your own genius?

Isaac Newton once said, "I consider my greatest accomplishment to be lifelong celibacy."

References

Science discovers the physiological value of continence, R. Bernard, 1957, pg. 23, 33

Research Study: Rosalind Arden, Linda S. Gottfredson, Geoffrey Miller, Arand Pierce
"Intelligence and semen quality are positively correlated."
Intelligence, Volume 37, Issue 3, 2009

You Are Acting Out the
Will of the Universe

It is said that we are the universe, becoming aware of itself. The universe experiencing itself through our own eyes. The powerful energies of the cosmos are circulating inside of us. Less than an ounce of this energy is enough to create new life.

When you are retaining your seed the content of the universe itself is accumulating and condensing it's energy inside of you. Much like the forming of a galaxy over billions of years, the universe within you powerfully expands.

The Taoist Master Mantak Chia once said: "Sperm is the storehouse of male sexual energy. (...) The manufacture of a sperm fluid capable of such psychic super potency consumes up to a third of a man's daily energy output.." (Mantak Chia, 1984, pg. 17)

The life force that grows inside of us when we retain puts us in tune with nature. Our experience of reality begins to shift. The universe will work hard to accommodate you. Opportunities start to come your way, people gravitate towards you. Your presence will affect other people on a deep visceral level. It sounds almost unreal, but every day new accounts of these experiences are written about through various retention communities. After abstinence, many have reported their lives drastically improving in many aspects, physically, mentally and spiritually.

The term "trust the universe" may seem cliche or overly spiritual, but there is a very practical element to this meaning. The universe wants us to evolve and develop. Evolution is its purpose. If we move in accordance with the laws of nature, then nature will guide us towards what we are seeking, this is a naturally occurring process.

Your powers of intellect, intuition, and life purpose will strengthen and increase exponentially. For monks and ascetics this evolution will be a spiritual one, for a businessman it will be in their field of work, for an artist it will be the ability to tap into the deepest creative powers available to man. Regardless of the field of life you are in, the build-up of your energy will nourish your brain, body and spirit. It will guide you. It will affect those around you too, they will sense your growing aura very deeply. Retention will, over time, propel you towards great heights of achievement. Many of the world's greatest men attributed their genius to sexual abstinence and semen preservation.

Nikola Tesla once said.. "I recognise the importance that sex plays in the life of man. Nature has made its attraction irresistible to insure the perpetuity of the race. As for myself, I have found that the thinker is confronted with the problem of perpetuating either the species or mind. Before I produced the rotating magnetic field, I concentrated all my powers upon my experiment. The strain would have killed a hundred oxen. I certainly could not have survived it if I had permitted my energies to be diverted into the channels of sex."

Preserving your seed is the secret to connecting yourself with the divine power of the universe. Over time you will undergo a transformation. You will vibrate at a higher frequency, attract new people, new experiences and delve into new realms of existence. Words don't go far enough to convey the deep significance found in sexual abstinence. It is as much a mental journey as it is a physical one. As much a physical journey as it is a spiritual one. They are all connected.

Experience it for yourself.

References

Taoist Secrets Of Love, Mantak Chia, 1984, pg. 17

'Nikola Tesla's Youth and Strength. Physical Culture, N.Tesla, George F. Corners, March 1935

Semen Loss and the Brain

According to R.Bernard, in the field of psychiatry, there is strong evidence of a definite relationship between the sex glands and the brain, and the degeneration of the latter organ is usually accompanied by degeneration of the former. (R.Bernard, 1957, pg. 18)

"You eject the substance of the synovial fluid [fluid in the joints]. You send forth, to gratify a moment's passion, the very material of which the brain is made. This is a fact which you will acknowledge when you consider that all this semen is the material of which all these substances are made and supplied, and when the semen is ejected you have selected the best part of the body to go out and become to you a useless inert mass, which can never be restored to you under any circumstances. It is lost and gone." (Keith, 1913, pg. 239)

Out of all the organs in the body, the brain and testes have over 13,000 proteins in common with each other; the highest number of common proteins of any two organs in the human body.

We have previously discussed studies that indicated higher sperm quality equates to higher intelligence. Perhaps the health and nutritional state of one of these organs may give us an indication to the state health of the other? There are various published studies that have linked sexual dysfunction with brain disorders.

Written in the 1850's, "Physicians and physiologists of all ages, agree in opinion that the loss of one ounce of semen is more debilitating than the loss of forty ounces of blood! "The seed of man" says Hippocrates, "arises from all the humors of his body; it is the most valuable part of them." The fluids from every part of the human frame appear to rush to the genital organs, to give greater effect to the first act of nature. All the powers of the body seem to be suspended, or rather concentrated to one point, during the time of coition. Galen says "When a person loses his seed, he loses at the same time the vital spirit; so that it is not astonishing that too frequent coition should enervate, as the body is thereby deprived of the purest of its humors." It has been described by Aristotle, as the excrement of aliments, having the faculty of reproducing bodies like that which produced it. Others have described it to be a portion of the brain, and have pointed out certain ganglions, which form the communication between it and the testicles. It is termed by Plato a running of the spinal marrow ; and by Epicurus, it is called a part of the soul and body. Pythagoras says it is the flower of the parent blood; and Alcoeon considers it a part of the brain." (Pancoast, 1858. pg. 63)

This connection should not be controversial at all. Perhaps we are somewhat aware of the testes/brain connection already. Even in the English language we have the expression "Think with your head and not with your balls." As if to imply that one can literally 'think' with their testicles. This connection of the sex glands to brain health has been documented in numerous studies. The official stance seems to be that it remains inconclusive whether or not semen loss has any negative effect on the brain, but based on the available research and evidence, the argument to abstain from ejaculation is quite convincing if one wishes to keep their mental faculties intact and full of vitality, far into old age. This seems to me the logical action to take. It is not for me to tell you how to proceed with this information, do with it as you wish. I'm only making you aware that the information exists.

References

M. Keith, The Marriage Law, 1913, pg. 239

Science discovers the physiological value of continence, R. W. Bernard, 1957,pg. 18

The Science Of Sex Regeneration by A.Gould & Dr. Franklin L Dubois, 1911, Pg. 4, 9, 33

Onanism - Spermatorrhea, S. Pancoast, M.D., 1858, pg. 63

Physical Regeneration

As a man you are gifted with a sacred instrument that can harness the vital energies of the universe. It can allow you to reach the heights of genius in your area of pursuit. If misused it will lead you to degeneration and destruction.

"The force that generates in the human body those elements which, when used in accordance with natural law, serve to perpetuate the race, is the same force, which, when recognised, properly understood and rightly used, will regenerate the body, strengthen
the mind, build up character and develop a true and pure manhood and womanhood." (Gould & Dubois, 1911, pg. 48)

What is vital energy?

"Vital energy is, so to speak, a qualitative feeling which persists even when the body may be very tired from physical exhaustion. It is something more lasting than the immediate accident of physical exhaustion; it comes more slowly, but persists longer than the momentary states of feeling. It is, as it were, the colour in which the world appears to the individuality, and hence has a far more direct effect on mental states than physical momentary weariness." (Source Unknown).

The semen we secrete from our bodies via sexual activity is the energy to create life. This is the same energy used to build and regenerate our own bodies. Why do we have the instinctual need to secrete this valuable energy even at the expense of our own organism's survival? Because propagation of the species (even at the cost of the individual) is mother nature's first imperative. In the wild we don't have endless options of mate selection and sexual stimuli via online pornography and dating apps. The modern man today is bombarded with sexual imagery and opportunity to stimulate his sexual glands.

If we look at the animal kingdom, in nearly all cases animals do not waste their seed for pleasure. They use it strictly for procreation. They don't consciously do this either, it is wired into their instincts. Their adherence to nature's laws is inherent in their physiology.

The dangers of sexual excess have been long known and talked about through the ages of human history. The previously quoted texts were written well over 100 years ago and there are even texts dating back thousands of years, warning humans of the consequences of sexual excess. This is nothing new.

Stop leaking your vital energy.

Before we can regenerate ourselves we must fix any "leaks" within us that are dissipating our energies. Sexual activity and its subsequent sexual secretions are a major source of this energy loss.

"There is a certain amount of humiliation and weakness which accompanies the (sexual) act; the sense of pressure in the vas deferens is gone, and consequently there is weaker innervation there. But it is after eight or more hours that the lassitude, and mental discouragement affect the individual; the "acute" occurrence of what is chronic in continued dissipation and consequent incipient dementia."
(Guthrie, 1900, pg. 167)

We have been given capabilities to momentarily experience one of life's highest physical pleasures, yet in exchange we must pay the highest physical cost, a portion of our life force. Regeneration of your body can occur when you stop this leakage. Over time your body will begin to accumulate proteins, lipoids, & other constituents that are essential to the nourishment of brain, nervous tissues and organs, down to the very cell and mitochondrial functions of your body.

Restorative function of the brain, blood, nerves, organs, bones, joints and so on have been attributed to this practice in various texts over history. Such deep health improvements will perhaps improve the more surface benefits which are commonly discussed among retainers such as increased vitality, confidence, strong eye contact, more energy, motivation and so on.

Regardless of the findings and points of views of these texts, you can always try it for yourself and draw your own conclusions. The best knowledge I have gained on the topic came form self-observation. Thirty to sixty days of retention should be enough to be able to gauge whether you are experiencing physical and mental improvements. It will take an extended period of time to regenerate deeper so keep your retention on-going if you wish to see the potential for deeper benefits. Many retainers note that improvements are generally experienced within the first month of semen retention.

If you wish to experience the regenerative effects of semen retention, try it for yourself.

References

The Science Of Sex Regeneration, A. Gould & Franklin L. Dubois, 1911, p. 48

Regeneration Applied, K. Guthrie, 1900, pg. 167

Semen Retention
The Entry Point

Every choice you make creates a different timeline that your future will travel towards. Our reality splits into different trajectories, and you follow the path of your choosing. The concept of parallel universes already exists in our universe, whether or not it is occurring in the physical sense, the mechanism is very much the same.

We make a choice out of the infinite pool of choices, and our destiny proceeds accordingly. Begin to realise you are already living in a parallel universe. The YOU from yesterday has already traversed an infinite number of timelines to arrive at your current point of existence. You are jumping into parallel universes every moment from one reality to the next, changing the trajectory of your life path with each step. The majority of these jumps will place you in a comparatively similar timeline to your previous one.

It takes a much bigger jump to enter into a distant timeline. The preservation of your seed is an entry point. An entry point to a far away world that currently doesn't exist for you. If you want to go there, you can, it's easy. Your seed carries the intelligence of Mother Nature and the blueprint of creation. If you let that force build inside of you, the will of the universe itself will grow too.

You are the vessel that will carry out its will, that is to say, your own will. You don't need to create a plan.

The grand plan is already coded inside of you.

All you need to do is preserve your seed, and let the energy accumulate. The passage of time will expand your life force and your next step will become clear.

Do not take lightly these words.

Trust the universe.

You are exactly where you are meant to be.

You elected to come here before you arrived.

The universe has given you just enough help along the way and kept you alive to carry out your work.

This is what you are here for.

To unlock your destiny.

Never forget you have been blessed with a sacred jewel.

Allow that power to grow and your life's purpose will be brought forth.

This is not new-age hearsay.

This is ancient knowledge.

Passed down through many texts over the ages.

You carry the powers of God.

Because, you *are* God.

Your Sacred Jewel

Your seed.
It is the most powerful substance known to man.
It contains the source of life.
A part of your soul.
And you keep it stored within you.
You are it's protector.
If you protect it well you are free to draw on its powers for the regeneration of your mind, body and spirit. Your seed wants you to be at 100% as it relies on your survival.
This is a symbiotic relationship.
Your seed is a powerful jewel within this universe.
To embody this jewel,
you must keep it inside your body.

Whilst death is the full expulsion of your remaining life force, a semen emission is a partial one. The French expression for "orgasm" *la petite mort (the little death),* sums this up quite literally.

Patterns in nature tend to repeat themselves. Patterns of growth and patterns of energy. We have documented a common sequence of growth such as the Fibonacci sequence, based on a ratio, that indicate the template of growth patterns in nature from plants, to insects, to storms, to the human body. The organisms that adhere more closely to this ratio are regarded as more beautiful and healthy. In order to develop fully in accordance with this sequence we must not impede nature's course of growth. The grand design of nature is coded within you. Wastage of your valuable jewel will create an energy deficiency in your body that may hinder optimal development.

In the ocean there are tiny waves, huge waves and all gradients in between. A small wave doesn't wield much power, and breaks with minimal effect upon the shoreline. A big wave can tear through anything in its path with unstoppable force. A tsunami is so powerful it can obliterate cities, and permanently change the shorelines of the earth. No matter what format, accumulated energy impresses its will upon the universe with incredible force.

We have known about the inherent value of semen throughout various branches of knowledge for thousands of years. From philosophers to sages, to many medical practitioners, the conservation of sex-force has been proclaimed as the key to human progress and evolution. The use of our reproductive energies has been shown in many studies to negatively affect lifespan.

The enriching and powerful benefits of retention cannot be stated enough. In the previous eras of history many doctors and scientists began documenting the benefits of semen preservation and warning against sexual excesses. It should be noted there did, and still does exist, opposition to the argument for seed preservation, it is perhaps best to view the research on the subject yourself before drawing a conclusion.

Even the top athletes of the world have been aware of this value and refrained from ejaculation for long periods before competition. How did so many branches of humanity from vastly different eras of existence arrive at the same conclusion?

"We have seen that the internal secretions of the sex glands stand at the basis of the individual's physical and mental vitality and that sex hormones are present in the external as well as in the internal secretions of the gonads. Many of the effects attributed to such hormones, as we have seen, are due to the physiological effect of reabsorbed semen. Conservation of semen means conservation of sex hormones and increased vigour, while loss of semen means loss of hormones and diminished vitality." (Bernard. 1957, pg. 1)

Perhaps our bodies are merely vehicles for the propagation of this sacred force. The more of it we carry within us, the more this special force will reward us. Protect it at all costs.

References

R. Bernard, The Secret Of Rejuvenation, 1956, p. 1

The Road to Manifestation

Starting a long term streak of semen retention is a journey that will change you. If you block the leaks of energy in your system then that energy will condense and accumulate exponentially. The surplus energy will be diverted to all areas of all systems in your body. This is why the benefits you receive will be so wide and beyond calculation. It is the very fibre of your being that is being transformed. The more energy leaks in your life that you patch up, the stronger you will become. With a passion and a purpose, this energy will direct itself into your life's work. The first thing you need to do is create a path leading from where you are now to where you wish to be; the specific details of your end goal, the steps that are needed. We will go over a blueprint.

Before you proceed with anything, you need a goal to aim for. Without this you are like a rudderless boat in an ocean, floating aimlessly. Decide what you want to do with your life. This is not difficult, it should come to your mind with ease. If you have absolutely nothing then there is nothing for you to transmute with your energies.

1. Write your goal down. Close your eyes and fantasise the goal for a few moments, write down any extra details that come to mind so that you begin to create a narrative. Make it as fun and extravagant as you wish. Remember the strength of your desire will reflect the level of your success, so amplify your desire as much as possible. Remember when you were a kid, and you created elaborate stories of adventure in your mind and imagination? This is a power that most of us forget how to use. This will help you visualise the future

that the practice of semen retention will propel you into. Do this step carefully and properly.

2. Once you have a story, you need to materialise it into your visual reality. Go out this week and buy a white board. With a white board you write down your top goal with a date under it signifying when it will be achieved by. Don't make it too late nor too soon. Don't make it more than a few years. The sense of urgency is important. Write down the exact details under the goal, i.e; how much money, what kind of car or house or partner you will manifest. The more details you add, the better. On the other side of the board write down 3-5 bullet points needed to achieve this goal. Under each bullet point write down the smaller tasks needed to achieve each bullet point. Break them up into small tasks that are achievable within a shorter time frame. You should now have a basic attack plan for your goal's attainment.

3. Put this white board on your wall where you will see it everyday. If possible, close to where you'll be doing your life's work.

4. If you haven't already, start semen retention. This will be the fuel to help you achieve these goals. During extended abstinence, retention will bring out many feelings inside of you. Some of these feelings will be negative and frustrating and many will be positive and enlightening. None of these feelings matter because you have resolved not to release under ANY circumstance. Emotional feeling and physical action will be disconnected in your mind for the duration of this journey. Remember that the origins of many success stories came from traumatic experiences or from deep dissatisfaction with one's life and a feeling to change it. Don't avoid the pain, it's part of the cure.

5. Come to terms with the fact that you will need to not release for at minimum 6 months. Don't view this fact as a weak person would, as something too difficult. Look at it as a call to action, an opportunity for you to enter a higher quality of existence. The truth is, your masturbatory habits are much like a blanket you use to shield

yourself from the emotional pain of the world. Sleep without the blanket. Lose it. You have no need or excuse to relapse. If you treat this suggestion seriously you will manifest your goals more quickly. Remember that. Your decision here divides you from the 99.9% of people who won't be able to retain long term. Do you want to become something great in this world?

6. Now start accumulating hours. After the first month you'll notice subtle changes in the environment and by the end of the first month you'll begin to feel deeper changes taking place in your biology. Ten days equals 240 hours. How many to a 1000? To 5000? Work it out. You've only just begun the process. At this point keep your head down and keep going. You are saving your reproductive energies and diverting them into the maintenance and regeneration of your own body. The regeneration of your mind. This isn't a myth, this has been established scientifically in animals. When animals refrain from reproductive activities, they have an increase in biological markers of health and longevity. (Kirkwood, 1977)

7. For the first month or two don't push too hard on the goal. Make sure you are seeing it everyday and giving it a bit of thought. Don't shoot yourself in the foot when not seeing immediate progress, you are in the early stages. This now established goal, coupled with the accumulating energy of abstinence will start to stir something deep inside of you. Remember you'll get negative phases too, this is an important part of your progress, because these seemingly unbearable times cause us to take action to improve our circumstances. The chain of events will unfold differently for each individual but as long as you are covering the necessary parameters you will be on the right path.

8. You now have a basic plan for reaching your success. You can either forget this and move on now or decide that this is the day you change your life. Are you happy to humbly accept a less-than-ideal existence or are you going to proceed until your deepest desires and dreams are realised? There are two choices here. Two kinds of

people that you can choose to be. Which kind of person you decide to become is up to you...

References

Kirkwood, T. (1977). "Evolution of ageing". Nature. 270 (5635): 301–304.

Magnetism & Aura

"Physicists have demonstrated with incontrovertible facts that it is eminently healthy to conserve the vital principle. The seminal secretion has a wonderfully immanent value; and, if retained, is absorbed into the system and adds enormously to man's magnetic, mental, and spiritual force. (…) Other things being equal, the man who wisely conserves is improved in concentrated mental and physical power and effectiveness, (…) He builds, and constructs, he is the organizer and executive head of industries, he is the orator and the inventor. He is the leader of great movements, because his power is drawn from an inexhaustible storage battery. (Dr. Stockham from the writings of Atkinson, 1922)

The quality of magnetism.
We feel it in the presence of particular individuals.
The way they move, the way they speak, the way they make us feel.
An uncontrolled ball of energy can well up from inside, just from being within range of one these magnetic beings. Their aura wields a natural force, much like an electrical current, that everyone in the vicinity instinctively feels. In watching their interactions we can see others fall deeply under the spell of their charm. In a group setting they appear as the star of the show, the life of the party, bursting with potent energy that everyone eagerly feeds off. It's difficult to quantify this visceral feeling with language. However it is a common enough phenomenon that perhaps most have experienced it at some point.

What is this magnetic quality that we are experiencing?

"It is one of Nature's unfailing laws that the best of her species shall possess the greatest powers of transmitting their kind; and who can for one instant, question the conclusion that vigorous sexual powers, temperately and legitimately used, actually brighten and strengthen a man's every faculty, elevate and inspire his every ambition, giving him greater influence and capacity for anything he may attempt in life. But few men by their own efforts have ever accomplished anything of value in life who were not gifted also with a strong sexual instinct…" (MacFadden, 1900, pg. 14)

The power of magnetism lies within our sexual nature. Over the last century many publications on this topic have attributed the power of magnetism to man's sexual nature. The desire to procreate builds up immense energy within us. When we don't allow this energy to be wasted, it develops into a potent force.

"If we wish to make a success of our lives, we must follow the plan of our divine creator
as he intended, and the most important of the lessons we have to learn is that of the
right control of the forces generated within."

"Bear in mind that by retaining these fluids you furnish the highest type of material for building perfect brain cells, as well as developing a magnetic attraction that consciously or unconsciously will impress all with whom you have dealings. The conservation of Sex Force (sexual vitality), will perpetually rejuvenate the Whole body and preserve your strength to extreme old age." (Atkinson, 1922, pg. 202)

We must become aware of habits that both regenerate and degenerate our body. Our body is in constant motion moving either towards growth or towards destruction.

"The importance of retaining the sexual power, of using it wisely and temperately cannot be overestimated. It is paramount. Lose your sexual power, lose the power to reproduce your species, and, according to the laws of nature, your days of usefulness are past, and decay and death will soon over take you. Impotence sexually means impotence in everything, impotence mentally, physically, socially, etc. Your powers are fast waning - you might just as well be laid away without further notice." (McFadden, 1900, pg. 14,)

"The most disagreeable of persons is the one who has wasted all of his vitality, retaining no magnetic force; the brain, being the greatest sufferer, cannot do its best work. Each one can prove this for himself by observing such men and women as are addicted to sensuous lives, who come under his notice.

Many geniuses, who accomplished Wonders in a few years and gave brilliant promise for the future, have suddenly found themselves deprived of their mental powers as a result of giving way to their sensuous nature, and it has been repeatedly proven that a sensual nature can not produce anything of lasting value. Such an ending to the upward flight of a nature which had early given promise of a high career, is sad to behold." (Atkinson, 1914, pg. 26)

If we enter into a state of regeneration our body will begin to build upon the more subtle qualities of our organism that contribute to the essence of one's magnetism. The energy in the eyes, the complexion of the skin, the vitality in the voice and all the other countless improvements that people subconsciously pick up on during their interactions that create this sense of enigmatic power.

"Where the conditions are such as these, a store of life energy is gathered in the body which throws out all worn-out atoms; sends new life into those that are exhausted; revivifies the brain cells.

Creation, Pro-creation, Regeneration thus provides a more efficient instrument for mental work, and generates a store of personal magnetism which inevitably draws to the individual the esteem of the people he deals with, as well as every good thing in the universe. This is the re-generative effect of the sex function, rightly, intelligently and purely exercised." (Gould & Dubois, 1911, pg. 149)

It seems the perspective of magnetism being intrinsically connected to sex force has been long held throughout the ages. The fact that so many separate publications have alluded to the same cause only strengthens the argument for preservation. If you wish to generate your own aura of powerful magnetism, try it out.

Retain your sex energy for 6 months and see where life takes you...

References

'Regenerative Power', Stockham as quoted by W. Atkinson, 1922

'The virile powers of superb manhood', MacFadden, 1900, pg. 14

'The Private Lessons In The Cultivation Of Sex Force', W. Atkinson, 1922, pg. 202

'The Science Of Sex Regeneration', Gould & Dubois, 1911, pg. 149

Life Force

Upon entry, we are given a human body and the means with which to control it. We enter this system as an avatar capable of moving through time and space. We are given the independence of thought and movement. A single being that is very powerful. One human body at maximum capacity has the ability to bend this entire system, to their own will. We have seen this with dictators, spiritual leaders and in others in positions of power where the point of influence to millions lies within one being. It only takes one person to irreversibly change the world forever.

That one part can affect the entire whole is testament to the power that one holds within them, and the whole has no interest in you changing it. Your body is an instrument of energy conduction, capable of wielding unimaginable levels of power. There are systems in place that seek to stop this from happening, to prevent an excess of power given to a single individual. A sort of algorithm that operates to prevent any movements that work to compromise the clutch of power that is being held over all entities. As time moves forward, this system, that has been in place for so long, is becoming known to humanity.

Interestingly enough, as the system works to consolidate its power over the whole, the whole is becoming aware of the system itself. Humanity is becoming aware of the forces that seeks to control it. This giant brain we are all inhabiting is becoming more aware of itself. Through the internet, the individual cells are gaining access to the source of human knowledge, and birthing what we refer to as AI. As the integration process of human to digital continues, soon everything that exists inside of our phones and computers, will exist all around us, in the physical realm that we inhabit. This process is slowly culminating into a single pin point of power, a singular event that will open a portal in to the next dimension, that we will all soon inevitably traverse through. The next level up of existence.

The world is awakening.

Any techniques that condense immense powers into a single entity or being give rise to an independent source of power within that individual. This power grants the individual a stronger capacity to physically manifest their will into physical form. When much energy accumulates within a single unit of space, the pressure within that space increases. If the structure cannot withstand the pressure, a leak is formed and the energy dissipates out into the ether. A balloon with too much air bursts, sun rays condensed through a magnifying glass burn, a nuclear device reaching critical mass causes a nuclear chain reaction. Condensed energy is a powerful force. It is the strength and integrity of the structure that determines how much pressure it can withstand, thus how much energy it can hold.

Semen retention works in such way that one can accumulate their energy inside of their body so that it regenerates them into a highly powerful state of life force. The level of accumulation depends on the individual's strength of will to keep these forces within their body without them being expelled. Sexual energy conservation is an alchemic process that has been discussed and practiced throughout the ages since ancient times.

R. Bernard attributed a continent life as the secret behind many of history's great minds such as Pythagorus, Plato, Beethoven, Newton and so.. As he explains, "They conserved their seminal lecithin which was converted into brain lecithin, providing their brains with optimal phosphoric nutrition, on which brain activity so greatly depends..." (R. Bernard, 1956, p. 2-3)

There is still much we are yet to learn about energy, so we see the benefits of retention expressing themselves in often abstract ways that appear almost unexplainable to anyone who hasn't tried it for themselves. One might find themselves receiving attention from people or animals, unsolicited offers from others, heightened intuitive awareness and so on. If you have ever seen sound waves in sand you will see that the patterns of sand are organised into completely different forms depending at which frequency they are vibrating. In much the same way you are raising an output frequency by abstaining from interaction with your lower energies. This change in frequency rearranges the entire state of your existence.

Your semen creates life. Your body is alive and in order to make new life it has to sacrifice a small portion of its own. Many people today are losing this valuable resource on a regular basis and when repeated over time, this has been said to deplete our overall life force. After the leaks of loss are stopped and the energy builds up within the body, one may feel immense emotional and physical pressure, coupled with a strong desire to release those built up energies via sexual activity. But once this leak of release is sealed up, the energy will seek to express itself in other ways, in more creative forms of endeavour. This is how transmutation occurs.

This energy needs to be expressed and it will express itself unconsciously in anything that you do, in any venture you undertake. It does not necessarily require any such special rituals to transmute this energy. All that is necessary is the habit of retention and the physical commitment to the objectives and activities you are carrying out. If you are an artist you just need to keep making art while retaining. If you're a business owner you just need to keep working on your business while retaining. It has been my experience that no particular transmutation ritual is necessary here. It is simply the physical act of carrying out your life's work whilst conserving sexual energy that will allow for transmutation to occur.

"A speaker or writer who is addicted to waste in this department, though he may talk and write with great profuseness, may expect that his words will be comparatively powerless in their effect upon others. They will lack germinating power. But he who retains this element, other forces being in proper balance, charges not only his words his but his very atmosphere with a power which penetrates and begets new thoughts and new emotions in those with whom he comes in contact. Reserve is the grand secret of power everywhere. And when the fit time comes to exercise the crowning function of manhood to impart the germ of a new immortal, who shall repeat oneself in a nobler type, to expand and rejoice through the eternities - he who has reserved his forces has at full command the elements requisite for the godlike purpose." (A.E Newton, as quoted in Karezza, Ethics of marriage by Alice B. Stockham, 1903, p. 101)

As an entity increases in energy, the power of the will increases accordingly. The body is an instrument of physical manifestation, the more energy in the instrument, the more force it is able to generate out into the physical realm.

Written over a century ago on the subject of semen loss…"But there should be no waste. It's too precious. It is the concentrated essence of all the life forces of your being, distilled and compounded with marvellous chemistry in the most wonderful of laboratories. These are not fine words merely they state a most undeniable fact. This element when retained in the system the mental powers being properly directed is in some way absorbed and diffused throughout the whole organism, replacing waste, and imparting a peculiar vigour in every part. It is taken up by the brain, and may be coined into new thoughts-perhaps new inventions-grand conceptions of the true, the beautiful, the useful- or into fresh emotions of joy, and impulses of kindness and blessing to all around. This, in fact, is but another kind or department of procreation. It is the procreation of thoughts, ideas, feelings of goodwill, intentions of truth, that is, it is procreation on the mental and spiritual planes, instead of the physical." (A.E Newton, as quoted by Stockham, 1903, p. 100)

Internally there will be more energy to replenish lost energy stores and increase the structural integrity of your physical being. This surplus energy will be directed towards the regenerating of your organism's brain and nervous system, bloods, organs and tissues. The process of regeneration is gradual and ongoing much like the process of degeneration. Once the leaks are stopped, the elixir of life that was constantly being lost is secreted back into your system to power every cell within your body. To make your brain and body young again.

"It has long been known that the principal sex glands, the testes, produce the sperm cells which are the vital constituents of the semen. The semen which is exuded from the body at different times is called external secretion. But it has only been very recently that it has been discovered that the testes have another very important work, that of elaborating an internal secretion which is absorbed back into the blood and carried to every organ and tissue of the body. It assists in the building up of bone, muscle, nerve and brain, and causes the higher characteristics of virile manhood to develop. Even at the present time, though the exact nature of this wonderful secretion of the testes, which is called spermine has not been determined, but the production by the testes of a substance having the wonderful influence mentioned has been plainly established.

It is easy to see the wonderful effect of these fluids in the youth and those that have lived continent lives have nothing but benefit to report from experiences. It is the secret of the wonderful transformation of the boy into a man. The powerful muscles, the vigor of nerve and brain, the manly form, the qualities of will, initiative and courage, idealism, the social instinct, sex love, etc., are all dependent for their normal development on the sex organs. It is a well known fact that through any cause the functions of the testes are destroyed before puberty, the essential characteristics of manhood take on a different form. They are likely to be completely without them, or only have them in a very minor form." (Gould & Dubois, 1911, p. 210)

Consider the transformational process a man goes through during the stages of puberty. The development of muscle and form, the growth of body hair, the deepening of the voice, the mental shift. An utterly metamorphic process of change taking place in large part due to the internal secretions of the male hormones from within the testes. From this process do we not witness first hand the indispensable value of the internal secretions and their necessity to the male human body?

Butler writes: "We consider the physical body as a chemical laboratory. The food we take into the stomach passes through various stages of transmutation in the process of digestion: first becoming chyle, then blood, when it is thrown into the generative functions and becomes seed; then the seed, through the action of the same functions, is changed to lymph — a transparent, colourless fluid. The word lymph is derived from nymph (spirit), and this fluid is therefore quite properly called spirit-water, or water of life.

After passing through these stages it then begins to affect the mental conditions, and as it is carried by the lymphatic system through all parts of the body, it causes a pleasurable sensation in all the organs.

The more the seed and fluids are retained in the body without waste, the greater fulness of life, health, and power is experienced by the person. If it were possible to discharge all this fluid, the body would soon die from blood-poisoning.

An abundance of this lymph gives a feeling of rest, happiness, and satisfaction under all circumstances, also physical strength and love of activity. This fluid aids in forming the bright red corpuscles of the blood, and also assists the lungs in their work of purification. A portion of this regenerated blood passes into the spleen, where the pure white corpuscles are formed; from thence the most refined elements are taken up through the nerve system into the brain, and there changed into the subtle element of thought-potency, giving power to mental action." (H.Butler, 1921, p. 14)

These restorative and regenerative benefits associated with conservation have been written about extensively throughout history in scientific books, medical books, biology books, philosophical and religious texts. Regions all over the world that had minimal contact with each other during previous periods still arrived at similar conclusions regarding the benefits of retaining one's sexual force. The link between the mind, the sexual organs and the connection to one's state of health have been recognised and discussed for thousands of years.

Few souls there are on this earth capable of containing the life force that stirs inside of them. A force that so desperately wishes to escape. It is the essence of creation that is flowing through your body and coursing through your veins.

References

R. Bernard, The Secret Of Rejuvenation, 1956, p. 2-3

A.E. Newton, as quoted in Karezza, Ethics of marriage by Alice B. Stockham, 1903, p. 100-1

The Science Of Sex Regeneration, A. Gould & Franklin L. Dubois, 1911, p. 210

Solar Biology, Hiram Butler, 1921, p. 14

Matrix Mechanics

Remember, "It is the mark of an educated mind to be able to entertain a thought without accepting it." - Aristotle (as quoted by Lowell Bennion).

None of these ideas should break your views of reality or existence, they are merely perspectives of reality that warrant further thought.

At this point in your journey if you are beginning to see how the constant cycle of ejaculation may be draining something from you, perhaps even intentionally, despite what you've been told by popular opinion, then possibly you are thinking more critically about this reality and not readily accepting the narrative you have been presented with. This puts you in a minority of people within this world. I'm not here to say ejaculation is wrong, just that if you hold the view established in biology that reproductive activity shortens lifespan, as expressed in the Disposable soma theory of aging, (Kirkwood, T.B.L. 1992)
then perhaps one may question the premise that constant ejaculation is without consequence.

A deeper layer to this that I think many on retention will eventually ponder is, why have we humans been set up in this way to be constantly releasing our energies? Why has it been so fervently encouraged?

There are billions of humans across the lands constantly releasing energy into the ether. On a macro level much energy is being transferred by this process. Is this energy we are harnessing and releasing going somewhere? Are we charging something? It could perhaps make sense that we are charging something, a system environment or a process, and if it is something that is being charged then could the reliance on our continuous energy output not be essential for that very system's own survival? Perhaps what is relying on our energy is the system of reality itself, the physical realm we are inhabiting may be reliant on our energy or perhaps our consciousness for it to exist.

There is a strong societal push to dissipate our energies into the ether. Perhaps this push to drain our energies is inbuilt into this system to encourage energy output? Strong influential forces exist in this world, in the media, public opinion, propaganda; they encourage certain beliefs and actions above others, and they play a central role in shaping public perceptions. One such example is the encouragement of the dissipation of energy through sex and masturbation. But if we view the world from a more mechanical point of view, these abstract forces may be nothing more than complex systems or algorithms of sorts that ensure maximum output of all the battery cells, or human energy cells. That we humans are generating electricity has been well established for many years. "The elements in our bodies, like sodium, potassium, calcium, and magnesium, have a specific electrical charge. **Almost all of our cells can use these charged elements, called ions, to generate electricity.**"

(How the human body uses electricity. (n.d.). Retrieved October 4, 2022, from https://www.graduate.umaryland.edu/gsa/gazette/ February-2016/How-the-human-body-uses-electricity/)

The inventor of the battery Luigi Galvani had conducted experiments where the legs of frogs suspended on brass hooks would twitch when prodded with certain metals, he referred to this response as 'animal electricity.'

We tend to see the world through the lens of spirituality, science, human relations, emotions, feelings and so forth, which gives us a sense of humanism and encourages us to feel that we are very different entities of existence than say a robot or a machine. Yet strip away all these these humanised aspects of the world and we are left with a sophisticated system of cells that reproduce, consume and output energy, a highly advanced system of energy conduction, much like a computer or a generator.

There is really very little we can definitively know about the nature of reality for the simple fact, that we are immersed inside of it. There is no point of reference where we are able to view this realm from outside of itself. We can't perceive up without down, we can't perceive black without white. A man born blind cannot accurately grasp the visual experience, even if it is explained to him verbally in depth by one who has the ability to see. For the man born blind, the concept of seeing is imperceptible. It is a door that cannot be opened. It cannot be explained with words, words do not suffice. It must be experienced first hand to be known. Like the man born blind, we can see how words and thoughts may fail us in trying to understand what lies beyond the veil of death. It is likely not an experience that can be understood with conscious thought.

Regardless of how or why we are here, we do know at present that humans exist in this realm and spend much of their time exerting energy and recharging. Our bodies harness and recharge energy for a time until we are no longer capable of doing so, at which time we expire. Our seeds that we have birthed into the world continue on the job of outputting energy. Humans not only harness energy physically but also mentally, through emotions and attention. We know that attention or observation changes the things we look at, perhaps even bring things into existence.

From the famous double slit experiment we have seen how observation collapses wave function from a superposition of multiple potentials to a single state, that is to say, pinned down into a state with a definitive value.

What this means is that before observation the state of things remains as unlimited potentiality and it is the very act of observing that locks it into place; that collapses reality.

This can make us question whether reality is actually existing in areas we aren't currently observing. If you are watching a girl in a house on TV, does the tree outside of the house at the end of the street really exist? The tree is not on the TV screen, (of course if you were to take the camera outside to view the tree it would be there but as the tree is not on the screen there is no data in the TV directly supporting its existence), so does it actually exist in that TV program or would it be necessary to be in front of the camera before it exists? The TV screen only uses energy to animate what's in front of the camera, it does not animate the entire surrounding universe inside of its circuits, it only recreates what the camera is being focused on. There is not enough data or energy to recreate the entire universe of everything outside of the current camera frame in view. To only bring into existence what is in front of the screen is optimal for energy efficiency, so as not to expend energy unnecessarily. It seems reality also operates in such a way. The double slit experiment may support this notion, that whatever is outside of the scope of the observer need not be forged into its physical manifestation until it has been directly observed. That is not to say that objects outside of observation have no relation to what's inside the frame, just that the physical manifestation of the unobserved object may be unnecessary and not physically existent. Rather, it may remain in a state of pure potential that requires observation to lock the reality into physical substance.

As the saying goes "if a tree falls down in a forest and nobody hears it, does it make a sound?" Does the sound exist without the observer to hear it? It seems that our interaction with reality is a prerequisite for the existence of that reality.

Many expressions in the English language have perhaps hinted at the energetic qualities of human attention. For example, "Where attention goes energy flows" and "Attention is the most important currency that anybody can give you. It's worth more than money, possession, or things."

Look around you. Reality is set up to harness human attention. Your phone that begs you to look at it frequently to check your social media, emails, applications and browsing; your television with its unending broadcast of entertainment endlessly clamouring for your attention. Before the advent of television and phones there were newspapers, magazines, paper ads. It is perhaps the case that such devices too are harvesters of human energy, serving some deeper purpose, of powering some larger process that we cannot perceive from this level of existence. Powerful forces appear to be extracting energies from the human to charge something much bigger than ourselves.

Because of this energy output that humans exert in all fields, we develop and evolve as a species in a particular way; towards a direction that we are not yet fully aware of. Soon humanity will fully integrate with A.I. and from then on to incomprehensible levels of evolution. Through this we may perhaps create a new world, with new perceptions, a new dimension that doesn't currently exist. Whatever the overall intent of this system is, the point that seems clear is that our human participation is absolutely necessary. This system or this reality seems to feed on energy for survival. That is to say that without the human energy input this universe may cease to be. Without our consciousness of this realm this realm may not in fact exist.

This reality is powered by your attention, by your emotions, by your energy. It feeds off them. Reality is a system that seems to feed off energy to function. As time goes on, technology improves and the overall output of human energy increases. Technology amplifies human energy output at an exponential rate. The level of information our computer chips now store would be unfathomable to previous generations of technology; the output of words, videos, all sources of information that in time help move the wheels of human evolution faster and towards advancement to the next stage of existence. It seems that as time continues, the energy requirements to power the functioning of this reality are ever increasing and the simultaneous evolving of technology caters to this energy demand.

All of your devoted attention and experiences throughout your daily life are intrinsically connected to the running of this system environment you inhabit. Reality is an illusory, virtual environment that is powered by human energy. It is obviously not the default state.

Reality is hard to define. The parameters with which we have been provided to understand life have their own limits. We have a brain that can observe connections and patterns and make overall observations based on these connections. Yet we cannot express with certainty beyond this point what it is we are actually perceiving. What is blue? A colour? It can easily be defined by the word blue. But does it really give us the truest essence of what blue actually is? What is blue? What is colour? Perhaps we can define it as not being red, not being green. By virtue of what it isn't we can establish what it is. But how can we get further down to the deepest unadulterated truth of what blue actually is? At this point, blue is just blue. Our human mind cannot take it any further than this. It has reached a limit of perception that may not move beyond that point. But there may be more to blue than can be comprehended by thought. There may be higher levels of knowledge that form the structure of reality that cannot be experienced by the human brain.

Something we do appear to see however is that we have a start point and an end point. An entry point and an exit point. A birth and a death. This could be indicative of a vacuum environment. And if we are really existing in a linear sense then perhaps we will experience a day when we will die. Such a concept could suggest that we are inhabiting some sort of enclosed system. Some sort of system environment that has been constructed to perform a particular function. Perhaps we are existing for a particular purpose. These are just concepts that we can consider among oceans of other ideas that are equally justifiable as to why we may exist. The notion that our perceptions of reality may be merely smaller, limited representations of what really exists out there, gives us a strong starting point to explore the nature of reality.

References

(How the human body uses electricity. (n.d.). Retrieved October 4, 2022, from https://www.graduate.umaryland.edu/gsa/gazette/February-2016/How-the-human-body-uses-electricity/)

Disposable Soma Theory of Aging, (Kirkwood, T.B.L. 1992)

Desire

What separates us from animals?

Self-awareness.

Between our instinctual urges, and our actions, lies the voice of reason.

If we can find a higher purpose, we are able to override our animal instincts.

We can hold an ideal in higher regard than the gratification of our senses. This is an ability that although within reach, few people can accomplish.

"It is but repetition of the conviction of the greatest thinkers and of the mystics and the spiritual leaders of all ages that for every person who wishes to advance in evolution and to attain real happiness there comes a time when "desires must starve . . the animal passions must die."

"Nothing hinders us so much in the development and exercise of our inner powers as . . . our external desires. (...) By transmutation the lower desires will automatically shrink, dissolve and vanish. Suffering will then yield its place to constant exaltation; for freedom from desire like the choicest extract from the choicest treasure. Divine influences will come to him who liberates his soul of all carnal desires." (Van Vliet, 1939, pg. 44)

We may be bound in this life to our physical senses, yet we need not be controlled by them. We are aware that we are a part of something bigger. Our perceptions lie within a limited spectrum of consciousness. The colours we see, the sounds we hear, the vibrations we feel, all have upper and lower limits of perception yet we know that there exist realms beyond those limits.

Birds, for example, have four colour cones in their eyes, whereas humans only have three; allowing them to see a much broader spectrum of colour. The fourth cone that humans don't posses allows birds to detect UV rays.

A wider range of animals can hear sounds that we cannot hear. Our frequency of audible perception is from 20hz to 20khz. A bat's hearing range is from 9hz to 120 kHz. Animals such as dogs, cats, mice, elephants, horses, dolphins and more are perceiving vibrations in this world that we are unable to perceive. They are living in a universe that we don't have access to.

Humanity and the self, are intrinsically connected. We can sense something that exists beyond our senses. It's difficult to quantify in words. We operate like some kind of cog in a complex machine. But paradoxically, that machine we are operating, is ourself.

When we realise that the good of humanity is for the good of the self, we can act in accordance with ideals that are beyond our base desires. Sacrificing our sensual enjoyment for a higher purpose is a form of evolution. When you stop chasing desire and start working towards a higher purpose, you gain support from the universe. When you conserve your procreative energies, they build up into a tidal wave of unstoppable force. This force is transmuted into your life's work which ripples throughout the universe, deeply affecting every cell, in every being in existence. We have seen this great power wielded throughout history by the greats, Tesla, Gandhi, Beethoven, Da Vinci. Their efforts have greatly shaped the world in which we live in today. If you wish to tap into this higher vibration of existence, of creative genius, then the control of your animalistic desires is of paramount importance. To achieve control over your own mind is the mark of true greatness.

References

'The Coiled Serpent', C.J. Van Vliet, 1939, pg. 44

Eyes Are the
Windows to the Seed

One of the most commonly purported benefits of semen retention is its effects on the eyes. The eyes are said to become clear and sharp; magnetic and charming after periods of sexual abstinence. Out of all areas of the body, why is it that the eyes are so often notably improved on retention?

Seminal excretions are said to tax the brain, blood and nervous tissues of vital nutrients and energy. A taxed brain will provide less support to the eyes, nerves and all other organs and tissues throughout the body. Eyes carry a direct connection with the brain via the optic nerve.

"The eye is connected to the nervous system, with the brain as the centrepiece of the system. When looking at how both organs function, the eye and brain show similar needs for nutritional support." (Healthysights.com, Accessed in 2022)

Out of the brain, nerves and eyes, it is the eyes that are most visible to the outsider.

Much biological information about the mental and physical state of the organism is transmitted through the eyes. For this reason the eyes play an important role in the process of mate selection. A potential mate can gauge much biological information from your eyes alone. It has been said before that eyes are the window to the brain.

Research has found various associations with the eye's functional integrity and brain condition. (Kumar V, 2018) Sperm production draws much of the same ingredients for nourishment and nutrition as the brain and nervous tissues. According to R. Bernard
on the topic of abstinence, the sperm and brain use much of the same resources, and thus, excess use of the former can lead to degradation of the latter by way of nutritional deficiency. (R.Bernard, 1957, pg. 37-42)

The eyes receive nutrition directly from the brain and nervous system. If sexual excess leads to under nourishment and degradation of the brain and nerves then this will have a tremendous impact on the eyes' state of health. There is perhaps a lot more that science will unravel about the brain, eye and testes connection. The key concept here however, is simple. We should be very aware of our own energy expenditure. It can be seen by others very easily, a lot more than you perhaps think. When you lose semen, the consequences are written all over your face and body. Be wary.

The more energy preserved, the more energy our body can put towards regeneration and revitalisation.

Preserve your seed and your body will have a strong supply of nourishment for all of the other parts.

Your eyes will shine and carry a magnetic quality that others will innately sense. This effect will contribute to your overall aura, and people will perceive this when interacting with you.

Semen preservation is a cornerstone of optimal health.

The benefits of conserved fluids will seep into every part of your being, right down to the last cell.

Try it for yourself.

References

Healthysights.com, 'Eye To Brain Connection.' Accessed in 2022
https://www.healthysights.com/en/kids-teens/eye-brain-
connection.html

Kumar V. Eye is the Window to the Brain Pathology. Curr Adv
Ophthalmol.
2018 Aug;1(1):3-4. doi: 10.29199/2638-9940/CAOP-101013. Epub 2017
Nov
15. PMID: 31123726; PMCID: PMC6528662.

Brahmacharya
& Taoism

Brahmacharya. "Many are the keys to health, and they are all quite essential; but one thing needful, above all others, is Brahmacharya. Pure air, pure water, and wholesome food certainly contribute to health. But how can we be healthy if we expend all the health that we acquire ? How can we help being paupers if we spend all the money that we earn ? There can be no doubt that men and women can never be virile or strong unless they observe true Brahmacharya." (M.Gandhi, 1921, pg. 70)

There are various schools of thought among cultures as to how sexual abstinence is practiced. The Brahmachari do not encourage stimulation from sexual thought at all. All thoughts and actions of a sexual nature are to be eliminated from consciousness.

"My dear brothers! The vital energy, the virya that supports your life, which is the prana of pranas, which shines in your sparkling eyes, which beams in your shining cheeks, is a great treasure for you. Remember this point well. Virya is the quintessence of blood. One drop of semen is manufactured out of forty drops of blood. Mark here how valuable this fluid is! " (Swami Sivananda, 1934, Ch.6)

The Taoists, on the other hand not only support sexual activity but have many Taoist methods and techniques for the practice of sex, however without the loss of seminal fluids.

"A person's approach to sexuality is a sign of his level of evolution. Unevolved persons practice ordinary sexual intercourse; placing all emphasis upon the sexual organs, they neglect the body's other organs and systems. Whatever physical energy is accumulated is summarily discharged [through orgasm], and the subtle energies are similarly dissipated and disordered. It is a great backward leap. For those who aspire to the higher realms of living, there is angelic dual cultivation [transmutation]." (Lao Tzu)

It should be noted that not all Taoists practice semen retention and some recommend a frequency schedule of ejaculation based on age, season and body constitution.

It could be extrapolated that the increase in sexual activity will lead to an increase in semen buildup in the prostate, and without an ejaculation, the body will need to excrete semen through the urine or resorb it back into the body. This process of excreting through the urine is commonly referred to as retrograde ejaculation. The amount of semen that is resorbed is not known, though many have proclaimed the benefits of resorbing semen back into the body.

This could perhaps indicate that Taoists resorb more semen than their non-sex practicing counterparts, the Brahmacharis. This resorption of semen is said to have a powerful regenerative effect on the body. But does it influence longevity?

It begs the question. If resorbed semen nourishes and regenerates the body, and eunuchs cannot produce semen, then why did eunuchs appear to live longer than semen-producing males? Are the benefits of semen retention due to the fact that our body doesn't work as hard to produce semen, or are the benefits of retention due to the regenerative effects of the resorption of semen back into the body?

This is an important distinction that hasn't yet found public consensus.

To my knowledge there are no comparative studies that have analysed such differences and therefore we have no definitive data to confirm this either way. The Taoist methods involve sexual stimulation and thus perhaps produce higher level secretions of testosterone compared to their non-sex practicing counterparts, the Brahmachari. From research we have learnt that increased testosterone negatively affects longevity. On the other hand, however, it is said that testosterone increases virility, aggressiveness and male secondary sexual characteristics.

Although we can scientifically quantify levels of testosterone produced in the body, we cannot quantify levels of "Ojas," which are said to be produced when practicing Brahmacharya. Ojas is a spiritual and energetic concept of vitality that cannot be measured scientifically. That is not to imply Ojas does not exist, but rather that it's substance may be too broad and profound to measure within a narrow spectrum of data.

At this point in time, coming to a definitive conclusion about which is the superior path, is a futile effort.

If you were not born into either of these philosophies then perhaps you can try both and decide if either lifestyle works for you. As we delve further into the subtleties of each practice, we move beyond the quantifiable realms of science and must rely on our personal observation to attain the best result.

Try them both, and proceed accordingly.

References

A Guide to Health, by Mahatma Gandhi, 1921, pg. 70

Practice Of Brahmacharya, Swami Sivananda, 1934, Ch. 6

Hua Hu Ching: The Unknown Teachings of Lao Tzu, trans. Brian Walker, (1992), Section sixty-nine

Do The Powers Stop
On Long Term Retention?

Many have reported that after long periods of semen retention their powers become less noticeable than when they first experienced them. They don't feel the same highs as they initially felt. They don't feel the same level of magnetism. And thus much doubt is cast on the effectiveness of their semen retention journey. Why does this occur?

It's perhaps safe to assume that the benefits experienced upon retention are a reflection of the increasing health markers and overall quality of the organism.

As we start retaining, many physiological changes begin to take place from within us. The prostate secretions of hormones such as testosterone and prolactin will inevitably vary once we alter our prostate activity. To my knowledge there is limited scientific research on human sexual abstinence beyond the three week mark, so detailing these hormonal shifts is outside the scope of possibility. But we can deduce from studies on human, animal and insect reproduction, that the use of reproductive resources has an inverse correlation to most health markers, length of life and integrity of the organism. Thus, one can quite clearly infer the benefits associated with semen retention.

Semen retention is the process of avoiding reproductive activities and preserving semen to accumulate abundant energy. Once we go long term on retention, our body no longer needs to constantly replenish lost resources from seminal emissions. With a surplus of energy, our body now has the resources to work on the regeneration of the organism.

Let's look at another form of energy abundance; riches.

When one who was previously poor suddenly wins or inherits fortune, what is the initial effect? Massive lifestyle change, euphoria, ecstatic feelings of joy from their new-found riches. The change is enough to shake their world to the very core. A self transformation occurs as they gain access to their every desire. But what is the common long term outcome of such cases? The eventual return to their baseline levels of happiness.

This phenomenon occurs so frequently that it has been researched and dubbed "The Adaption Level Theory." Research has been conducted on both lottery winners and accident survivors. (Brickman, 1978) This research concluded that regardless of either winning the lottery or experiencing sudden misfortune, people generally returned to a baseline level of outlook and happiness. We know the cliche that money doesn't buy us happiness, but it does provide us with the tools to achieve a rich and fulfilling existence.

Most wealthy people will attest to this. Ask a rich person if they would ever give up their wealth and return to their previously poorer state. The answer will be an unequivocal and emphatic "No!"

Now, how does this apply to semen retention?

It is important to note that a person's first experience of the benefits of retention will perhaps give them a sense of euphoria and joy, (much like the lottery winners upon receiving their fortune.) A newfound sense of confidence, feelings of vitality, a clearer mind, magnetism and so on. The polarity from their former existence can be jarring. This euphoria will surely settle as time passes and one becomes accustomed to this new level of living. As we acclimatise, the previous buzz from the benefits will become the new normal. We won't get the same buzz or feel the same "high." As we get past the initial "high" we may even feel that our magnetism was much stronger previously. We may even begin to doubt the effectiveness of this journey and feel the temptation to relapse. Remember there is always a voice in your head that will try to justify your relapse. Make sure your concerns regarding long-term retention are not influenced by that voice that wants you to give in, that wants you to release your seed.

Whilst we will go through ebbs and flows over the course of our abstinence, the overall direction of our progress can be nothing but upwards. A return to our former habits would only be a step backwards. The biological cost of reproduction and semen loss is undeniable. The retirement of reproductive and sexual faculties is known to extend lifespan in plants, animals and humans. Research has concluded time and again the effects that reproduction has on shortening lifespan. It is a widely accepted pattern in biology. The final result of the act of reproduction and masturbation is essentially the same, an ejaculation causing the loss of vital seminal fluids.

Upon consideration of the long-term effects of reproduction on the organism, it seems that restraint of the sexual act will be more beneficial for the purpose of maintaining our organism's health and longevity. The supposition that the benefits of semen retention wear off is quite contrary to the research regarding the reproductive cost of the lifespan. If you are starting to doubt your journey after a few months, give it more time. Your body is adjusting to the changes and dealing with a new way of living. A few months is not a sufficiently substantial length of time for any deep biological regeneration. You need to be patient. Give yourself a year and then look back on the benefits. The results of your efforts will become undeniable.

References

Brickman P, Coates D, Janoff-Bulman R. Lottery winners and accident victims: is happiness relative? J Pers Soc Psychol. 1978 Aug;36(8):917-27.

Semen Retention
The Circadian Cycle

If you are practicing semen retention, you are walking a path that very few on earth choose to walk. You are sacrificing one of man's most enjoyable pleasures in order to amplify the life force energy from within you.

If the regeneration of your body and life force energy is of great importance to you then you'll make semen retention your first priority.

But this is not enough. If you wish to elevate your powers and regenerate your body further, then it is absolutely necessary to follow the circadian cycle that is coded in your DNA.

Semen retention is the generator of your life force whereas your Circadian Rhythm is the regulator of your energy. It diverts the accumulated energy to your bodily systems at different times and plays a vital role in many biological processes such as sleep cycle, hormone secretion, cardiovascular health, body temperature regulation, glucose breakdown and so on. The optimal regulation of these biological processes is what prevents our body from developing serious illness and disease. If we are to avoid premature mortality, cancer, diabetes, and degenerative illness, then our circadian rhythm must be strictly adhered to. If we are to maintain youth, amplify aura and develop stronger magnetism then we must abide by our Circadian Cycle.

In short,
Early to bed and early to rise.

This is how to live in accordance with nature.

Melatonin

Whilst sleeping in the dark, our body produces the hormone melatonin. This hormone helps to regulate the sleep cycle, and also plays many key roles in the maintenance of organ and cellular function. "It is believed to be originated to protect the unicellular organisms from oxidative products which were emerged from aerobic respiration. (…) melatonin acts on cellular homeostasis by regulating the main molecular mechanisms that sustain life and control death,..." (Kuwabara, et al., 2022).

Melatonin also regulates the cell's mitochondrial function. It is said that the nucleus and mitochondria of cells contain the most melatonin. Mitochondrial dysfunction and degeneration is known to contribute to cellular senescence, chronic inflammation and the overall process of aging.

Much like semen retention, following your circadian rhythm is another key to harnessing life force energy and regenerating your body. These two practices coupled together will fundamentally transform you. Optimal energy generation and regulation is what we should be aiming for. It is of no exaggeration to say you'll experience super powers. Your aging process will slow down, your rate of cellular regeneration and maintenance will increase, as will the sharpness of your mind. Just about all observable health markers will greatly improve.

When we follow the designated sleeping patterns of the sun, we are following the rules that nature has set out for us. When we follow the rules nature has set out, we are awarded abundantly. This must be our ultimate goal. To live in accordance with the natural laws of the universe, brings us into harmony with existence itself. The transformative powers of this small habit cannot be overstated. Following this rule is absolutely essential. Every area and function of our body will improve dramatically if we adhere to this simple principle.

Sleep time must take precedence over all else. I know it sounds to many like an impossible sacrifice, but take a strict approach. That work that needs finishing after midnight, sleep now and finish it at 6am. Realise that if we view sleeping early as a luxury and not a necessity then we are doing so at the expense of our organism's biological integrity and overall quality of life.

If utmost health, utmost aura, utmost attractiveness, utmost energy is your priority, if you wish to max out your body to its full strength and capability, then adjusting your sleep timing to the rhythm of nature will become your top priority. If you can do retention for a week, then you can sleep early for a week. The benefits of these two practices together will accelerate your progress and put you well on the way to achieving your life's purpose.

References

Kuwabara, W., Gomes, P., Andrade-Silva, J., Soares Júnior, J., Amaral, F. and Cipolla-Neto, J. 2022. Melatonin and its ubiquitous effects on cell function and survival: A review. Melatonin Research
. 5, 2 (Jun. 2022), 192-208.

Semen Retention
The Alchemy of Thought

What is money?
Money is paper.
Paper with numbers printed on it to represent value.
What makes it powerful?

A long time ago a group of people created this product and convinced
all the other people alive that their paper, and their paper only,
contained value. The owners of this product could print any amount of
this paper at any time. Money now controls the world.

How did this come to be?
Where does the power in all of this lie?
Belief.

Money is valuable because we believe it to be. If everybody
simultaneously refused to recognise its value, it would instantly be
rendered worthless. The power of belief is real.
Many people perhaps don't realise this but when they believe in
something they are transferring a portion of their own energy into the
existence of that object. We are all aware of this on some level, it's why
we take to heart the beliefs of others, even at the expense of our own.
This ancient knowledge has been known and used to set up some of
the biggest institutions in human history.

It is not that we believe things because they are true.

It is that things become true because we believe them to be.

That is how the universe works. And most of the world doesn't seem to recognise this fully. Most people don't seem to be aware of the infinite powers that lie dormant inside of themselves. Inside of you. These powers can be activated at any time. Your body is an electrical receiver that can harness accumulated energy to manifest anything from the outer realms into the physical plane. Into reality. it is perhaps impossible to conceptualise what we humans really are from an outside perspective, but there is much more at play here than what meets the eye. We have no frame of reference to objectively see something we are incapable of separating ourselves from. We are in too deep. The universe is inside of you. It's what you came from. You have grown from the universe and are now manifesting its will. Your will. You are it.

You create anything and everything you believe to be true. Much like a sculptor using the raw materials of reality to sculpt his art into the physical form. This world is but a dream.
One third of your lifetime is spent existing in dreams which are worlds much like this one created by your thoughts and beliefs.

Over 2000 years ago, the Chinese Philosopher Chuang-tzu wrote:

"Once upon a time, I, Chuang-tzu, dreamt I was a butterfly, fluttering hither and thither, to all intents and purposes a butterfly. I was conscious only of my happiness as a butterfly, unaware that I was Chuang-tzu. Soon I awakened, and there I was, veritably myself again. Now I do not know whether I was then a man dreaming I was a butterfly, or whether I am now a butterfly, dreaming I am a man."
- Chaung Tzu

Think for a second. What is a dream?

It's stimuli that your brain is interpreting.

But then, what is reality?

It's stimuli that your brain is interpreting.

So what is the difference?

A dream appears unreal from the perspective of reality, but how does reality appear from the perspective of a dream?

Your existence here is far beyond the limits of your own perception. There are infinite dimensions that are existing within us. Everything that you believe to be true can be materialised into this world. Humans carry the ancient ability to perform alchemy.

Every invention on this planet was once previously an intangible concept, in the mind. Our bodies pulled these ideas from the ether and into existence. Our bodies are that powerful. You have within you the power to materialise anything you want. All you need to do is visualise it. Fantasise about it. And feel it deeply, like when you were a child.

Become aware that you have this special ability. You manifest things into reality with your beliefs, so treat it with the respect it deserves, and acknowledge the power that exists within you. If you can truly understand this, it will become a very powerful tool for you in this world. So many of us have forgotten how to use this ability.

Within this understanding comes the most vital seed of knowledge.

You are god.
This world and everything in it was created by you.
Without you here, this all ceases to exist.
I'm not really here.
Nor is anyone else.
It's just you.

Semen Retention
Extends Life

To get closer to youth,
We must move further from death.
What does death entail?
The ultimate destruction of the organism due to gradual or sudden physical degeneration.

Before we consider regeneration we should perhaps first focus our thoughts on the reduction of degeneration.

As the saying goes "A penny saved, is a penny earned."

It is widely known in biology that a major cause of aging and accelerated physical degeneration is reproduction.

From encyclopedia.com:
"Reproduction generally reduces survival, more reproduction shortening life span, less reproduction increasing life span. This effect is not absolutely universal, but it is one of the better established patterns in the biology of aging."

Reproduction is carried out through the physical act of mating. The biological result of this process for the male is the production and secretion of semen from the sex glands and subsequent ejaculation of said sexual fluids.

The act of masturbation carries the same biological end result for the male, that being the secretion and ejaculation of semen. From observing the physical mechanisms of mating and masturbation, it could reasonably be concluded that the end biological result of these two activities, are essentially the same. Assuming that the costs of reproduction are based on the loss of these fluids, which is evident, it would be reasonable to surmise that the act of reproduction would bear much the same biological effect and consequences on the organism as the practice of masturbation.

The esteemed British psychiatrist Charles Mercier wrote; "The function of reproduction has by its very nature a disintegrative deteriorating influence upon the organism in which it occurs...the reproductive act has an effect on the highest regions of the nervous systems which is of the nature of a stress, and tends to produce disorder.
(...In the male) the repeated loss of energy eventuates in a state of energy, apathy, lethargy and dementia. The tension of energy in the nervous system is reduced to the lowest ebb, and all the manifestations of the existence of this energy are wanting or are exhibited in a feeble and perfunctory shape. The condition is one of dementia ... there is want of mind, the inability to perform mental operations of even moderate difficulty, the dullness and slowness of feeling, the loss of all higher emotions and of many of the lower ones also characterise dementia." (Mercier, 1890, pg. 234)

From this line of thought we can establish that the first rule to be followed for longer life is that of reduction of lustful thought, sexual activity and most importantly, the avoidance of ejaculation of the seminal fluids.

There is evidence to suggest that an 'elixir of youth' may actually be present within the chemical constituents that make up the semen. The chemical make-up and consistency of the semen is of a very similar make-up to that of the brain and nervous tissues. Both the brain and semen are made up of numerous elements including phosphorus (lecithin), lipids, cholesterin and a particular substance known as spermine. It has been suggested that the brain and sex glands are in direct competition for the use of these substances and that overuse of one gland will cause deficiency in the other. Sexual excess may in fact have a very direct negative influence on the brain and nerve's ability to access these vital constituents.

If conserving the sexual fluids within our bodies is to equate to longer lifespan then we could assume these substances as being very beneficial to overall longevity. Claims of the powerful effects of these substances on longevity were made over 50 years ago. Recent research has concluded that spermidine indeed delays aging in humans. (Madeo F, et al,. 2018)

That we can absorb this elixir of life by means of preservation, for free, without the need to go out and spend hefty sums of money for its acquisition is perhaps a miracle. An overlooked miracle. A deeply significant health secret that we currently all have access to.

We are all slowly dying, but at different rates. Reproduction accelerates our rate of degeneration and ultimately leads to earlier death. The key is restraint. Restraint of sexual activity in order to activate regeneration via the absorption of the valuable substances produced and secreted by your glands. To furthermore save energy stores in the body by stopping the regular loss of semen which would require constant replenishment. Is this something you are prepared to sacrifice? It is by no means a requirement and for some, the enjoyment of sex makes life all the more worth living even at the cost of their own lifespan. These are all philosophical questions that one must ponder and reach a conclusion for themselves. Our values are all different. But if you desire to hold on to your youth and vigour, well into old age, then the avoidance of reproduction is of great importance.

References

'Longevity: Reproduction' https://www.encyclopedia.com/education/encyclopedias-almanacs-transcripts-and-maps/longevity-reproduction, Accessed in 2022.

'Sanity and Insanity', C.Mercier, 1890, pg. 234

Madeo F, Carmona-Gutierrez D, Kepp O, Kroemer G. Spermidine delays aging in humans. Aging (Albany NY). 2018 Aug 6;10(8):2209-2211.

Semen Retention Attracts Hate.
Don't Take it Personally.

Semen retention in the long term inevitably leads to success. Practicing the art of semen retention changes your position in the projected social hierarchy of others, as your integrity deepens and your new-found competence becomes undeniable. For many, semen retention becomes the catalyst for a deep transformation of the self. When you perceive this transformative power it is often quite extraordinary. People around you will need to come to terms with your ascent. This is a hard pill to swallow for many close to you, particularly those that are within or hovering closely around your own perceived social status or rank. People don't like to have their sense of reality challenged and your journey of transformation is threatening to the very fabric of their existence.

When someone who once viewed you as an equal sees you raise your vibration to a higher frequency, this can have a very strong impact on their own sense of self; others may essentially question their own place in the social hierarchy. The deepening of your value, attractiveness and position can be taken as a personal attack on their identity. People form much of their own self-image based on a hierarchical scale with regard to others in their environment, and map out for themselves an imagined "level" where they stand in this world in relation to those around them.

Everybody around us gives us a frame of reference with regard to ourselves. To see someone else succeed can enhance our own feelings of failure. To see someone become more attractive accentuates our own perception of our lack of attractiveness. We are not individuals but parts of a whole, and when other parts of this whole exceed our own performance, it can reflect badly on our sense of self-worth. The co-worker or friend seeing you succeed may feel personally threatened by your actions. Your success has brought to attention their own lack thereof. People may even feel motivated to pull you down for this reason. This phenomenon is widely known as the "crab mentality."

This way of seeing the world is ingrained to some extent in all of us, and inevitably we will face this at some point on our journey. The light of others can feel like it is outshining our own light.

Being aware of this phenomenon should allow us to resist taking the negative actions and behaviours of others seriously at all. It is not personal. Remember the "you" that exists in other people's minds is not "you" at all. It is a separate character that they have formulated in their own mind based on a shadow of you. They may villainise or pedestalise that character at any time and you should know that it bears no relation to your existence. They are living in their own universe, playing their own game, so don't get involved in their universe. Realise it is a separate and inaccessible dimension to you.

Everyone wants the acclaim, the success and the glory but most are not prepared to sacrifice anything for it. Seeing someone like you, who has taken control of their own power, is a cold reminder of their own shortcomings. It is not about you, it is about them dealing with their own deep sense of dissatisfaction and helplessness in life.
Any unwarranted attack on you is a one-sided argument that the attacker is having with his own ego, there is no need to get involved. No emotional response is needed. They are screaming at a character on a TV screen, inside of a universe that you don't even inhabit.
Let it go.

Semen Retention
Pure Thought

Moral thought leads to beauty.
Moral thought enhances beauty.
Pure thoughts create a pure mind.
A pure mind creates pure habit.
Pure habit creates a pure body.
A pure mind in a pure body; that is health.

The attainment of true beauty and personal magnetism will require the cultivation of pure thought. Your thoughts are not as well hidden as you may think. Over time, impure thoughts can manifest themselves physically in the body and become etched into the character of the individual. This can have a negative effect on your interactions with others and the world around you. If people realised that the consequences of impure thought were so detrimental to their very being, they would never have an impure thought again.

The successful implementation of semen retention over the long term is no easy feat. It is an extremely rare achievement to retain the seed for years at a time.

The elimination of impure thought is the next level up. It is existence at a higher frequency. It is the retention within retention that will take you to the loftiest heights of human experience.

Perhaps for many practicing semen retention, the commonly held belief is that if fluids are not lost through ejaculation, then no energy is lost.

But even from the spark of a lustful thought, the prostate can activate and start moving fluids up the vas deferens in preparation for ejaculation. At this point it is already too late. It is said that semen can be lost and excreted via the urine from merely having a lustful thought. Although anecdotal, retainers have claimed to have cloudy urine or noticeable semen excretion via the urine after practicing edging or non ejaculatory sex.

From 1874, a published doctor's account of his patient:

"A young man who had visited the East Indies twice, as supercargo of a vessel sailing out of Boston, consulted me two years ago in regard to a "sexual nervousness" as he called it. He told me that while he had kept a native mistress in the East Indies, he had never indulged himself excessively, and yet he felt that he was losing his virility. He had become engaged to a beautiful woman, but feared he should prove unequal to marital duties.
The symptoms, as I thought, indicated a masturbator's exhaustion, and I told him it was best to speak freely, concealing nothing; that I was not in the habit of compromising any one who consulted me confidentially, etc.
He said, "I never practiced masturbation more than five times in my life, when my mother began to suspect something, and talked to me in such a way that I never was guilty again."
I then proposed to examine his urine, and to that end brought in five long test tubes, directing him to fill them in my presence. I saw nothing unusual with my naked eye, and after a time proceeded to scrutinise the sediment with a microscope. Discovering nothing of interest, I finally asked him if there was anything in his sexual life which he had concealed from me. "Nothing that I know of said he, "except that I indulge in thoughts about women. During my long voyages I have given myself a good deal to such things. I have taken with me a score of French novels, in which sex has been treated in a very fascinating way. Certain passages in these books I have read over and over, and then I have indulged for hours and days in thoughts to which such reading naturally gives rise."

"Have you observed after several hours abandonment to such fancies that your nervous system was greatly exhausted?"

"I have constantly observed it. I have noticed that intercourse with my Indian girl did not exhaust me half so much. But, sir, it is impossible to control my thoughts. Such fancies will haunt me, and it is impossible to get rid of them."

I then said, "Come to see me again in two days, and I will prepare in writing the course you are to pursue."

I advised him to eat very plain, unstimulating food, dispensing with supper altogether, and to work himself to fatigue every day (...) But I urged, above all other duties, the importance of keeping the mind free from impure thoughts.

Upon his return from another voyage, a few months ago, he called to see me. His face told of improved health, and as soon as we were alone, he began about "My great victory." "Cleaned out, sir. I wouldn't go back again to wallow in the mire for my life. And now I am going to marry, and I shall marry the woman's soul. If I had married two years ago, it would have been her body. What an animal I was !...." I have the impression that the service I rendered that gentleman was really more precious to him than to have saved his body from the jaws of death." (Lewis, 1874, pg. 33-35).

As we can see from such experiences as above, it is not only for purity's sake that we must think pure thoughts, it is for the purpose of conserving our energy, and maintaining a healthy physical existence.

Further writings on this topic from the 1880s help to illustrate this point:

"It is a wide-spread and deadly error, that only outward acts are harmful; that only physical transgression of the laws of chastity will produce disease. We have seen all the effects of beastly abuse result from mental sin alone.

"I have traced serious affections and very great suffering to this cause. The cases may occur at any period of life. We meet with them frequently among such as are usually called, or think themselves, continent young men. There are large classes of persons who seem to think that they may, without moral guilt, excite their own feelings or those of others by loose or libidinous conversation in society, provided such impure thoughts or acts are not followed by masturbation or fornication. I have almost daily to tell such persons that physically, and in a sanitary point of view, they are ruining their constitutions. There are young men who almost pass their lives in making carnal acquaintances in the street, but just stop short of seducing girls; there are others who haunt the lower classes of places of public amusement for the purpose of sexual excitement, and live, in fact, a thoroughly immoral life in all respects except actually going home with prostitutes. When these men come to me, labouring under the various forms of impotence, they are surprised at my suggesting to them the possibility of the impairment of their powers being dependent upon these previous vicious habits." (J.Kellogg, 1881).

Perhaps it's best to think of semen retention as not the end goal, but as a vital component to the foundation of a pure life. Purity is not just a mental concept. It manifests deeply within the fibre of your very being, influencing all who make your acquaintance.

References

Chastity, D. Lewis, 1874, pg. 33-5

Plain facts for old and young, J.Kellog, 1881, pg. 170

Beyond Retention
Restorative Benefits of Nature

Those practicing semen retention are cultivating health.

Whether it is your intention or not, the practice of retention is putting you on a path of increased longevity. As a by-product, your rate of age is slowing and you will stay looking and feeling younger for longer.

Are you practicing semen retention for the purpose of health, beauty and longevity? If you are, then semen retention is not the end of the road. If you would like to excel in these areas then it is necessary to apply yourself to all practices that cultivate health and beauty.

To live life in accordance with nature is health.

The qualities of nature are all conducive to good health. Nature is fresh air, sunlight, fresh water, natural sights, sounds and movement. These elements combined help our mind and body to reach a healthy state of equilibrium. As we know, semen retention is one of the tenets of good health, but it doesn't stop there.

"I can affirm, without the slightest hesitation, from my own experience as well as that of others, that sexual enjoyment is not only not necessary for, but is positively injurious to health. All the strength of body and mind that has taken long to acquire is lost all at once by a single dissipation of the vital energy. It takes a long time to regain this lost vitality, and even

then there is no saying that it can be thoroughly recovered. (...) the preservation of our vitality is impossible without pure air, pure water, pure and wholesome food, as well as pure thoughts." (Mahatma Gandhi, *1928, pg. 57*)

Many of us in today's world are severely disconnected from nature. We live in large boxes made from synthetic and often toxic materials that block out the sun's natural rays, shut off the earth's natural flow of oxygen and discourage bodily movement by way of chairs, sofas and beds. Spending ample time inside can significantly reduce our oxygen intake, reduce vitamin D and melatonin synthesis, increase toxin intake and bring our circadian rhythm into disorder. These are all states that hasten the degeneration of our organism.

The Sun Bath

"Sunbathing antedates recorded human history. Savages, "primitive" peoples, little boys and animals instinctively seek to avail themselves of the benefits of sunshine. There has never been a time when mankind has not enjoyed its influence and only a false ascetic pattern of life and the monastic ideals ever, even for a time, deprived part of the race of at least occasional use of the sun." (Shelton, 1950, pg. 332)

"Life is a sun-child," says Dr. Oswald. "Nearly all species of plants and animals attain the highest form of their development in the neighbourhood of the equator. Palm trees are tropical grasses. The python-boa is a fully developed black snake; the tiger an undiminished wild cat. With every degree of a higher latitude, Nature issues the representatives of her arch-types in reduced editions — reduced in beauty and longevity, as well as in size and strength." (Dr. Oswald, 1885, pg. 79)

Without the sun the body cannot function properly let alone at its optimal state, and over time this will lead to organism degradation. The sun helps to carry out many biological functions of maintenance and

127

synthesis within the body that are necessary for optimal health and vitality.

The regulation of mitochondrial function, cardiovascular improvement, bone health, the production of melatonin and synthesis of vitamin D in the skin, there are numerous known and many lesser known benefits of sunlight that make it an essential tenet of good health. It is of course advised not to over-expose yourself to avoid the many consequences of sunburn, but moderate sun exposure has shown to be of essential benefit to the body. During the early 1900s in the UK vitamin D deficiency was causing rampant illness particularly among the young:

"When you put the vitamin D story into the perspective of human history, it begins with the Industrial Revolution. As the revolution began to sweep across northern Europe in the mid-seventeenth century, doctors reported seeing a new disease that afflicted young children with a constellation of physical signs and symptoms, (...) What was happening was that as people began to congregate in Great Britain and northern Europe, they erected cities whose tightly placed buildings closed off to sunlight the alleys where kids were hanging out and living. Compounding the problem was the gathering pollution from coal burning, which thickened the air and blocked the sun's rays. When these kids started to show signs of bone deformities, doctors began to take note." (Dr. M. Holick, 2010, pg. 8)

It is my belief that the benefits of sun exposure vastly outweigh the negatives, though I recommend you research this topic thoroughly and form your own conclusions.

The Air Bath

Being outdoors gives direct exposure to the outside air, which even in most cities is infinitely fresher and more physically restorative than breathing the indoor air of a confined living space. It is not only the breathing in of fresh air but the fresh air contact with your bare skin that is of great benefit.

Written in the early 1900s:
"Nearly everyone is agreed today that sickness and short life are the consequences of unnatural and unhealthy modes of living. All are confirmed in the belief that fresh air is an all powerful source of health, and that bad air, on the other hand, is exceedingly harmful, even dangerous. These things are common knowledge, but how uncommon it is to find practice in accordance with the knowledge! The vast majority of people live in bad air. Good air, be it cold or warm—is the foundation of all conditions of life; bad air—cold or warm—is, everywhere, the most powerful and common cause of sickness and short life. (...) ..be in the fresh air as much as you can, to make a point of exposing the naked body to the fresh air and sunlight in your bedroom if you cannot do it in the open, to rub the skin and wash it so that it can perform its natural functions (the vital importance of which are generally overlooked) with freedom and ease; and to exercise all the muscles of the body so that you have a sound frame, strong in every part." (J.P Muller, 1908. preface & pg. 22)

The benefits of regularly exposing our lungs and body to fresh air are profound and numerous.

Studies have drawn the connection between low levels of oxygen and the proliferation of cancer cells. Some studies go so far as to label hypoxia, that is lack of oxygen, as the prime cause of most cancers. (B. Peskin, 2008)

The practice of exposing the bare body to outside fresh air was known historically as an air bath. In 1934 Shelton wrote "Benjamin Franklin was in the habit of taking air baths each morning in his room. He made some efforts to induce others to adopt the practice and speaks highly of the benefits he derived thereof. Franklin particularly desired to divest himself of all clothing when doing mental work..."

"Air playing over the body may increase metabolism fifty per cent in ten minutes. Thyroid extract, medicine's only claimed stimulant of metabolism, is said to require a year to accomplish this same thing. An air-bath of twenty minutes duration reduces the hydrogen-ion content of the blood to normal. No drug method known can do this in any length of time."

"Dr. Trall considered the air-bath as admirable in cases of scrofula, rickets, and other conditions. Rikli declared: "Man is made to live in the open air; therefore when exposed to the action of light, air and sun, he is in his real element."

"As soon as people realise that sun and air-baths are more important than water-baths, all of our cities will have public sun-parks where the people may go and take their sun and air-baths." (Shelton, 1934, pg. 81).

The Water Bath

Submerging the body in water, the traditional bath, has long been known for its many health benefits. In Japan, bathing is practiced daily and has been a part of the culture for thousands of years. Japan also has one of the highest life expectancies in the world. Studies have indicated various health benefits for people practicing bathing regularly. It is said baths exert hyperthermic action that induces vasodilatation and increases the flow of blood and thus oxygen and nutrients to the body. Some of the reported benefits of this practice regularly are: cardiovascular improvement, breathing and lung function improvement, stress reduction, hormone regulation, brain and nervous system improvement, blood and overall immunity enhancement. It may not be possible for all people but if at all possible, the addition of water baths will be of great benefit to to your overall health and appearance.

References

Self Restraint V Self Indulgence, M.Gandhi, 1928, pg. 57

J.P Muller, 'The fresh-air book', 1908, Preface & pg. 22

'The Sun Cure', W. Goodridge, H. Shelton, 1934

The Science Of Fasting, H.Shelton, 3rd Ed.1950, pg. 332

Household Remedies, Oswald, 1885, pg. 79

The Vitamin D Solution, M.Holick, 2010, pg. 8

Peskin BS, Carter MJ. Chronic cellular hypoxia as the prime cause of cancer: what is the de-oxygenating role of adulterated and improper ratios of polyunsaturated fatty acids when incorporated into cell membranes? Med Hypotheses. 2008;70(2):298-304.

Excess Ejaculation
Ugliness

What is ugliness?

We are all born with different body constitutions and levels of health. Some of us have stronger constitutions whilst others have weaker ones. We all inherit different sets of traits which reflect differing levels of general health, inherited physical characteristics and in other cases susceptibility to illness and deformity. These are the parameters of our existence, given from birth. From this point on however, we have the freedom to select many of our own life habits that will deeply influence our levels of health and physical appearance over the course of our lives.

Whether you were born into the top echelons of aesthetic beauty or whether you were born "unattractive" with physical deformities, it is best not to take any of it personally and to wholeheartedly accept whatever human body you've been gifted with in this life.

Many people may feel that their appearance has made their life more difficult than their more 'beautiful' counterparts, but try this change of perception; you may very well be playing this game of life on a higher difficulty level than that of your peers, and if that is the case, you must rise to the challenge and embrace it. Much like a video game, playing on hard mode can be a much more satisfying challenge and can ultimately make you a better player. You may not realise this but the pain of your struggles will deepen your appreciation of success and the experience of life itself.

To quote the famous Carl Jung: "No tree, it is said, can grow to heaven unless its roots reach down to *hell*."

When you've been down to the darkest depths, then the success of life is all the more sweet. Many who are born into riches never get to develop an appreciation of their wealth. Be thankful. If you've been given difficult circumstances, appreciate life at this level.

Moving on.

Regardless of wherever you were placed on the spectrum of aesthetics there is much you can do to move your marker either up or down the scales of attractiveness.

It has been discussed at length in various texts over history that semen loss via reproduction or masturbation leads to organism degeneration and the inevitable manifestation of physical unattractiveness. Modern research conversely indicates that attractiveness can be used as an accurate indicator of general health. It is perhaps necessary to make the connection between health and physical aesthetics so that we can see how the destructive habits that lead to to degeneration are also the roads to unattractiveness.

Centuries before, the renowned Swiss physician Tissot on the topic of semen wrote: "We may form some idea of its importance by observing the effects it produces; when it begins to form, the voice, the countenance, and even the features change; the beard grows, and the whole body often assumes another appearance, since the muscles become so large and firm that they form a sensible difference between the body of an adult, and that of one who has not arrived at puberty. All these developments are prevented by debilitating the organ which serves to separate the fluid producing them. Correct observations prove that the extirpation of the testicles, at the period of virility, causes the loss of the beard, and the return of an infantile voice. Can we doubt, after this of its action on the whole body, and not perceive the many bad consequences with which the emission of so precious a fluid must be attended."

Hoffman has seen the most frightful symptoms ensue from the loss of semen. "After long nocturnal pollutions," says he, " the patient not only loses strength, becomes emaciated and pale, but the memory is impaired, a continual sensation of coldness affects all the extremities, the sight becomes dim, the voice harsh, and the whole body, gradually wasted ; the sleep is disturbed by unpleasant dreams, does not refresh, and pains are felt like those produced by bruises." (S.Tissot, 1832, pg. 5, 11)

Let us now look at some possible factors contributing to this view of semen loss and it's influence on our state of attractiveness.

1. Reduction of lecithin, lipids and other essential nutrients, minerals and fats. Lecithin is a known ingredient of semen. With less access to lecithin due to semen loss, the body is less efficient at restoring lost levels which will over time take its toll on the condition of the organism. Lecithin is a necessary component for carrying out many vital functions within the organs of the body. "In view of the richness of the semen in lecithin, cholesterol, phosphorus and other constituents of nervous and brain tissue, it is clear that it is incontinence, or loss of these valuable nerve-nourishing substances which, by promoting undernutrition, is responsible for disturbed functioning of the nervous system and brain, and never true continence, contrary to the unscientific views of the psychoanalysts." (R.Bernard, 1957, pg. 1). Lecithin is found in all cells throughout the body and one could imagine that the deficiency of such an important nutrient among the many others could only be detrimental to the overall integrity of the organism.

2. Hair loss is often referred to as a symptom of the aging process and a sign of physical degeneration. For many, this process occurs much before deterioration from aging is scheduled to occur. It is well established that hair loss is related to sex hormones, in particular DHT. There are numerous factors that perhaps indicate a relationship to

excess ejaculation: Women do not produce or excrete semen and cases of alopecia in women are far less frequent than in that of males. In studies on Pomeranian dogs with hair loss after being castrated, the majority of the dogs re-grew their hair back at significant rates. (Huang, Lien, Chang, 2009). Historically, eunuchs who didn't produce or excrete semen never went bald. Also a common side effect of the most popular hair loss medications cause low libido, and such a reduction in the sexual appetites, as in the previous examples, seems to be correlated to hair health. It appears logical that the avoidance of ejaculation or at least, excessive ejaculation, can only have positive benefits for the hair. Please reach your own conclusions on this point as there is not yet an established official consensus on this relationship.

3. As biologists confirm that reproduction and reproductive activity reduce lifespan then it would follow common logic that before leading to an early death, the process of degeneration would be accelerated first. As masturbation and mating both end in the physical result of ejaculation and loss of semen, it seems likely that the negative physiological effects of 'reproductive activities', at least for the male, would also apply to masturbation. If masturbation does indeed reduce lifespan then it can be more than reasonably assumed that one would undergo an accelerated aging process before succumbing to an early death. Such an aging process may prematurely induce the commonly recognised symptoms of degeneration that are associated with "ugliness." These are all controversial perspectives, so do your own research before arriving at any concrete conclusions.

4. Spermidine has been researched and concluded to maintain telomere length and delay the aging process. In a study on humans, the cause of spermidine's life extending effects were hypothesised as follows: "Spermidine may counteract the general clock of aging, by a global effect on cellular fitness, or may exert specific effects on multiple organ systems engaged in for example cardiovascular function, anticancer immune surveillance or neuro-degeneration and thereby reducing the incidence of the major age-related diseases."

"Recent epidemiological evidence suggests that increased uptake of spermidine with food also reduces overall, cardiovascular and cancer-related mortality in humans." Madeo F, et al., 2018)

Taking into consideration the above reasons, there appears to be much merit in the avoidance of semen loss to ensure optimal maintenance of the organism and thus prevention of the degenerative processes that lead to aging and the subsequent state of unattractiveness. It is to my knowledge the actions of preservation of the organism that will most optimise your attractiveness potential. Before making an opinion on the topic you can try it for yourself and see if you benefit from the practice of semen retention.

References

'A treatise on the disease caused by onanism', S.Tissot, 1832, pg. 5

Science discovers the physiological value of continence, R. W. Bernard, 1957,pg. 1

Huang HP, Lien YH, Chang PH. Effect of castration on hair re-growth in Pomeranians with hair cycle arrest (alopecia X). J Vet Sci 2009; 1: 17–19.

Madeo F, Carmona-Gutierrez D, Kepp O, Kroemer G. Spermidine delays aging in humans. Aging (Albany NY). 2018 Aug 6;10(8):2209-2211.

Charisma

What is charisma?

Perhaps all of us have felt the presence of a charismatic individual before. Something inherently attractive and convincing in the way they talk, the way they move and the way they make us feel. Charisma is a somewhat abstract quality that is not easily nor rationally defined. Charismatic people emanate a strong energy that exerts influence and generates a visceral sense of magnetic attraction. It is a highly potent form of attractive energy that is not exclusively connected to the common physical markers of beauty.

Hitler, Gandhi even Donald Trump; regardless of your feelings towards these individuals, they each wielded the powers of charisma and captivated many in a powerful way, exceeding that which went beyond any manifestation of their physical appearance. They harnessed energies that entranced and influenced millions to follow their agenda. The energy that these people carried is a life-force energy. A sex energy. These powerful figures have all been known for their strong sexual natures, as have many of the world's most influential leaders.

Research conducted on the levels of sexual desire in people regarded as charismatic concluded that they do feel higher levels of of sexual desire than the average individual. (Tu, E, et al. 2022).

Self-help author Napoleon Hill said "Sex energy is the creative energy of all geniuses. There never has been, and never will be a great leader, builder or artist lacking in the driving force of sex." (N.Hill, 1937, pg. 168)

Perhaps this was why so many of the geniuses throughout history conserved this vital energy.

Why is it that some people experience higher levels of sexual desire than others?

Sexual desire is widely thought of to be positively correlated to testosterone. There is a lack of published research on long-term sexual abstinence and testosterone levels, however in recent years numerous users in the retention community have shared their blood test results before and after going on long-term semen retention. These results have indicated significantly higher levels of testosterone in the blood after long streaks, much more so than prior to commencing retention.

It appears that semen retention could significantly boost testosterone levels. Testosterone levels are positively correlated with sexual desire and mating success. Increased sexual desire has been correlated to increased charisma. It has also been said that "...High T (testosterone) is also considered to be a marker of genetic quality..." (Sánchez-Pagés, et al., 2009. pg. 5)

Conversely, scientists have found that mice on a caloric restrictive diet, experience both lower levels of testosterone and lower levels of attraction from the opposite sex. Although this is not definitive evidence of testosterone being responsible for attractiveness it does perhaps suggest further evidence of this correlation. (A. Govic, et al., 2008, pg. 140-6)

It stands to reason that semen retention could enhance one's charisma via the increase of testosterone levels attributed to long streaks. There is nothing concrete or definitive here, yet we could reasonably assume, along with the various testimonials on semen retention forums that have indicated a T increase in their lab results post retention periods, that there is perhaps a significant connection between sexual abstinence and increased charisma. In my own experience too, it seems that every long streak was accompanied by an increase in my receptivity from others, social influence and ultimately, level of charisma.

As the well-known Indian philosopher, Osho said: "When energy goes upward you will be more sexually attractive to others, because life energy going upward creates a great magnetic force. You will become more sexually attractive to others, so you will have to be aware of this. Now you will attract persons unknowingly, and the attraction will not only be physical; the attraction will be etheric." (Osho, 1970).

When you are practicing semen retention people will feel your presence. People will approach you more. Animals will approach you more. Babies smile at you. Energetic magnetism occurs beyond any scope of reason or rationality. Barring rivalry, many interactions become more positive. You may be approached more frequently for assistance, advice or even just directions. The unconscious desire of people to connect with you will increase by merit of your sexual energy conservation. You will attract higher vibrational beings and situations into your life. Something about you becomes undeniably magnetic. They see it in your face, in your eyes. they hear it in your voice. Without you even realising, your words will carry more weight. Your rivals will find it very hard to deal with! Your opinions will naturally exert a stronger influence on those around you. This physical realm is controlled by the life force. Those with more of this force exert more power. Those with less of this force wield less power. Those who can carry this practice on longer term will gradually emerge as supremely powerful forces to be reckoned with. They will enter the ranks of the great sages, artists and leaders of the world. With such an amassed power one will be able to manifest whatever it is they want in this world.

Humans respect energy. Abundant sex energy manifests itself in all that is beautiful, from the song of a bird to the feathers of a peacock, to the beauty of an artist's masterpiece. They are all manifestations of this life force energy. This sex energy. Conserve this sacred energy and your life force increases. The very essence of your existence will strengthen and its power becomes undeniable to all.

References

Tu, E., Raposo, S. & Muise, A. Leading Better Sex Lives: Is Trait Charisma Associated with Higher Sexual Desire and Satisfaction in Romantic Relationships?Arch Sex Behav51, 505–519 (2022)

N.Hill, 'Think & Grow Rich', 1937, pg. 168

Sánchez-Pagés, Santiago & Turiegano, Enrique. (2009). Testosterone, Facial Symmetry and Cooperation in the Prisoners' Dilemma. Physiology & Behavior. 99. 355-361. 10.1016/j.physbeh.2009.11.013.

Antonina Govic, Elizabeth A. Levay, Agnes Hazi, Jim Penman, Stephen Kent, Antonio G. Paolini. Alterations in male sexual behaviour, attractiveness and testosterone levels induced by an adult-onset calorie restriction regimen,Behavioural Brain Research, Volume 190, Issue 1, 2008, Pages 140-146,

Meditation & The art of ecstacy, Osho, Talks given from 1970, PDF version, pg. 122

Semen Retention:
The End Point

There will come a time when you have absorbed enough of what you need to know to master semen retention and integrate it successfully into your life.

If you feel you can continue this practice without the payment of conscious attention, then perhaps it is time.

That is to say, it is time to move on..

What does this mean?

Once you embody and master this habit of semen retention then it can be practiced without the application of conscious thought.

The habit of semen retention gives you an increased ability to achieve success in life. But it is not the object of success itself. The success lies outside of semen retention and inside the field of your life's work. The habit of semen retention creates a very powerful force, but especially so when melded with a pursuit of your undertaking. Semen retention should accompany your journey and not become the journey itself.

Making retention your central life focus can be a productive goal up until the point you have firmly absorbed the teachings. Eventually there is an inevitable point of diminishing returns. To invest too much time into the study of it will of course hinder the pursuit of your life's work which also requires much energy and study. If you have not yet reached a point where you can carry out retention unconsciously then you should persist with learning. If you have not yet absorbed enough of the teachings then by all means keep on studying. Find the resources from anywhere that you need. They are all available if you seek them out.

But know that there comes a time when you must graduate from this period of education, embody it in your life and free your conscious thought for the pursuit of your life's work, because this is why you are here. That time does not have to be now, but be aware that this time will, one day, eventually come.

If you are ready, then it is time to invest your valuable energies into your life's purpose. Your steadfast adherence to this practice will continue to pay dividends into your life without focusing conscious attention on it. What do you want to do with your time on this earth? This is all a game you have elected to play.

Can you sum up your life's work on earth in one sentence? Try it. Your ears hearing you verbalise this purpose will take immediate effect. It will strengthen your vision and prepare you right down to the cellular level for what needs to be done to achieve your outcome. Remember, your body is a powerful energetic instrument that materialises energies into the physical plane. This is an important step. Write your mission statement down and say it to yourself so that it can audibly enter deep into your brain. With semen retention you have the blueprint to achieve genius. But the blueprint is not enough. You need to start the real journey. Semen retention is the super car you can use on your road to success. But keep in mind, you still need to drive the car. You still need to start your journey into your chosen field. Much like an artist who has mastered their craft over many years, every stroke of the brush is made without conscious thought of all the techniques they have developed. The technique becomes ingrained in the subconscious and guides the hand accordingly without particular thought. Once the way of semen retention is firmly established within you it is time for you to move on to the act of creation.

This is what you were made for.

This is where your life awaits.

If the practice of retention inspires you then by all means continue to follow deeper down the paths and branches of knowledge. But for some or perhaps many of you, semen retention is not the end goal. Success in your field and progress in your life is perhaps the ultimate goal. For those people, much energy will be required to take action towards those goals.

You know how it works, you know the benefits too, but at some point you must start the climb from the bottom of the mountain. The rest of your life is a journey up this mountain. You have received a secret treasure that will help you tremendously along the way. It will put you far in front, provide you with much stamina, make you stand out from the hordes of lost souls. You will amass untold powers with your guarded gem. Those around you will instinctively feel the powers you wield as you continue this path and climb the mountain towards the peak of your life's work.

SEMEN RETENTION SUPPLEMENTARY COURSE WRITINGS

A selection of my course teachings and other writings of old to help you achieve success with Semen Retention

Part 1

Welcome.

This course was made to help you learn self control.

And, most importantly, to help you maintain semen retention long-term, if that is what you want to do. We are going to go down a rabbit hole of semen retention knowledge. Semen retention is not a new fad that came from the NoFap movement. It has existed since ancient times. Our collective history has much experience with sexual restraint, continence, chastity, semen retention - another name for the same practice. In this course I'm going to share with you some of the most interesting and most profound knowledge on this ancient practice, from times past.

I will be selecting the most pertinent information to help you realise how to practice self control. Refraining from your sexual nature is no easy task, and if you have decided to start on semen retention, then I trust that this course should give you enough knowledge, insight and perspective to make your journey a successful one. I am going to do the best I can to get this valuable information to your brain in the most powerful way possible. Remember however, at the end of the day, YOU will need to make the change. YOU will need to practice the discipline. YOU will get to experience first hand the many purported benefits on semen retention.

So as this journey begins, I wish you well, patience, and if you ever fall off the horse, remember to get back up and try again.

If you are having trouble with maintaining long streaks of retention then your problem comes down to a single point. You care more about five seconds of pleasure than you do about anything else, including the very essence of your own life force. You are forsaking your life, much like any other drug addict, for the sake of a few short-lived moments of pleasure. The costs are simply too great to be ignored, yet here you are ignoring them, wondering why everything is going wrong.

If you have spent years wasting this energy, perhaps you feel some regret. But keep in mind, this curse is reversible, or at the very least, a situation that can be dramatically improved. So many men previously have wasted their seed, and for longer than you, with worse consequences, so appreciate that you have found this information, as many have not.

This is a universal problem of man. A problem that all men go through and most men struggle with. They know that something is amiss when giving in to to their animal instincts on a regular basis. Most people can sense that something is off, something is depleting. A negative shift, a dullness, a deterioration. Something that is both mental and physical; perhaps even spiritual.

The reason you continue to forsake everything you know for a few seconds of orgasmic pleasure is simple. You don't understand what you are sacrificing with each loss of sexual fluid. You are unaware of the nutrients your body, your organs, your blood and your nerves have sacrificed in order to produce that valuable elixir that you are willfully ejecting from your body for the sake of a few seconds.

From now on, do not think of the word orgasm or come, rather, think semen loss.
Because that's what you are doing.
Losing semen.
Semen is the latin word for seed, ie; "that which is sown." It is the source from which life springs.

You are losing your seed.

As said by Vandana Shiva, "Seed is not just the source of life. It is the very foundation of our being." (Shiva, Ch.10, 2014, pg 236)

With every ejaculation you are losing the precious materials that brought you life.
You are sacrificing a small part of yourself for the sake of creating another human being.
And if you are not using your seed to create another human then you are a simply sacrificing yourself.
Yet in spite of this awareness of what you are losing, you continue to willingly lose the seed from your body; to wither yourself away into the ether, into nothingness. "...the destruction of the organism by imperceptible degrees..." (*Source Unknown*)

To commit this act of semen loss, even though you know its destructive force, is making a statement to the universe about who you are, as a person, as an entity.

You are the entity that cares for naught but your own self-satisfaction. You are thus rendering yourself a self-serving entity, that is of no use beyond the satisfaction of your own desires. What use does the universe gain from such an entity? Nothing. Yet you wonder why the universe is not providing for you?

Paradoxically, the more you put into this self-serving ritual, the less of you there will be in existence. You are literally shooting out the essence of what you are, through your penis, and losing yourself in the process.

The universe itself through various processes has amalgamated some of its energies into the entity that is you in order to further serve the evolution of this universe. Yet you are choosing to release those amalgamated energies into nothingness.

See how the universe is operating here? Things that don't serve the universe and only serve the self, inevitably wither the self away into nothing. What is not needed in the universe will eventually cease to be. That is why you must change your ultimate objective. Become an entity of value in this universe and the value of your entity will become supported and strong in this plane of existence.

If you were an employee in a large company, every day stealing money, every day satisfying your own ends and not working towards the betterment of the company in any way, eventually your behaviour would become known. Perhaps not the following day or the following week, but inevitably the time will come. The company will find no use for you and you will stagnate, receive no promotional advancement and eventually be terminated. Such is the pattern with the universe we are in. You are here to serve the universe. To aid in its advancement and evolution. Serve it you must.

The willing loss of your fluids dissipates your physical value, dissipates your mental value, and ultimately weakens your spark of existence in this realm. A complete and utter waste of your gifted energies. This is because the energy you inject into your own sexual self-fulfillment takes away from the potential energy you could invest into evolving this universe through productive work of some kind.

You become a weaker node of energy in relation to all the other nodes of energy. You become a smaller flame, a duller light, a weaker spark. Conversely, retain these energies inside of your body and something truly magical begins to happen. Your energies build, they magnify, they multiply and over time your entire being becomes more full of vitality, more full of energy, more full of beauty, and more full of life. Often without one's own conscious recognition, the conserved energy injects itself into everything you are and everything you do. It radiates from your core. The quality of your work, the quality of your physical being, the quality of your thoughts, everything is improved dramatically when the leaks of energy are stopped. Results inevitably are ensured. If you are conscious of it, you will feel it within yourself, and after a time, people around you will begin to feel this change too, this quality about you. You have direct access to the source of life itself, because it flows within you. The source of life, the seeds of genius, the antithesis of death. You become the source of power that everybody so desperately wants to be.

Now flashback to your current state of continual wastage.

Do you fully understand what was just said?

How are you continuing to dissipate your invaluable seeds of life and all that they bring, for the sake of a few pangs of excitement? What an unthinkable waste! You are experiencing life as a human now! You should be eager to live! Eager for life! How could you keep up the practice of draining your life seed, emptying out your life essence, merely for the sake of a few seconds of temporary fun?

Well, you are but one of the billions of men in this world doing the same.

That you are here reading these words is a sign that you are waking up.

You have sought out an end to seal the leaks of your life force, and here you are.

Regardless of any words I have to say, realise your journey has already begun. You have taken steps to put a stop to your energy loss. The wheels are already in motion. Your journey has already started. And I look forward to spending a short part of it with you, sharing with you what I've learned from others along the way through this practice.

References

The Vandana Reader, Vanada Shiva, 2014, Chapter 10, pg. 236

Part 2 - What are you losing? What is semen?

In order to seal this leak of energy that we have become so accustomed to wasting, let's delve into the specifics of exactly what it is that we are losing.

The seed. A seed contains the substances to create life itself. The source of everything that we are, and everything that we have come from. A seed holds the very essence of existence within it. How could expending such a precious ingredient inside of us be seen as harmless, and non-consequential?

From the words of H. Butler: "We consider the physical body as a chemical laboratory. The food we take into the stomach passes through various stages of transmutation in the process of digestion: first becoming chyle, then blood, when it is thrown into the generative functions and becomes seed; then the seed, through the action of the same functions, is changed to lymph — a transparent, colourless fluid. The word "lymph" is derived from "nymph"(spirit), and this fluid is therefore quite properly called "spirit-water," or water of life. After passing through these stages it then begins to affect the mental

149

conditions, and as it is carried by the lymphatic system through all parts of the body, it causes a pleasurable sensation in all the organs. The more the seed and fluids are retained in the body without waste, the greater fulness of life, health, and power is experienced by the person. If it were possible to discharge all this fluid, the body would soon die from blood-poisoning.

An abundance of this lymph gives a feeling of rest, happiness, and satisfaction under all circumstances, also physical strength and love of activity. This fluid aids in forming the bright red corpuscles of the blood, and also assists the lungs in their work of purification. A portion of this regenerated blood passes into the spleen, where the pure white corpuscles are formed ; from thence the most refined elements are taken up through the nerve system into the brain, and there changed into the subtle element of thought-potency, giving power to mental action." (Butler, 1921, pg. 13)

We have all been taught at length the benefits of healthy eating for good nutrition and body maintenance, yet at the same time we do not think even for a second about the release of our most nutritive substances from our body, our semen. How do so many claim this activity to be harmless? Does any of this make sense at all? Where is the logic here? If nutrition is so important then why do we only focus on the extraction of nutrition from food and not the preservation of our most nutritive sources and fluids? When you have the feeling to release, consider the cost you'll be paying to let go of such a nutritive precious substance that is working to regenerate and maintain the integrity and health of your body. Is a few seconds of pleasure worth such a vital loss of energy? Unless your efforts are not going towards the creation of a new human being then perhaps it is fair to say that the sacrifice is too great. The return is too small for such a substantial loss of vital energy.

References

'Solar Biology', H.Butler, 1921, pg. 13

Part 3 - Physical Preparations

If you don't own a calendar I strongly recommend you buy one.
Put it on your wall.
Somewhere easy to see.
Every day you successfully retain, put a star or draw a cross over the day.

Build the days up until you have an unbroken chain of days.
This is a popular method used for being consistent with tasks.
It works especially well for retaining your energy.
In my own experience it has proved very successful.

Try it.

It won't cost you much.
If you have expended the effort of following this course then go the extra mile and get yourself a calendar, hang it on your wall and log your progress.

Making your journey visual will help you immensely, don't overlook this point. For every day conserved cross off a day and see how many days you can get in a row. Your first challenge will be perhaps two or three consecutive days, then go for a week, two weeks, a month, and so on. See if you can keep going up until three months, and if you pass that milestone, six months, and then of course, the attainment of a year unbroken.

The art of retaining takes time and nobody is perfect. In my own case I started using a calendar in 2018 yet didn't commit to a full year until 2022. Yet those four years were filled with a six month streak, some three to four months streaks, some two month streaks and multiple month-long streaks.

Take it one step at a time, you will get there eventually. The benefits you experience along the way will only motivate you further to the next level.

Avoiding relapses

A relapse is when you are attempting to retain your essence but give in to temptation and masturbate to ejaculation. Edging is simply when you masturbate but not to ejaculation.
I want you to consider your schedule. Do you have scheduled days at home alone for long periods with no plans or human interactions?

This is dangerous.

Long periods of alone time with no one around seems to induce the desire to masturbate.

If you would like to avoid these relapses then it is wise to break up your "alone" days. Once you become fully aware of the physical effect semen loss has on the face and appearance you will perhaps feel less inclined to engage in the activity on days you have to interact with people, thus if you insert human interactions on your days with no interaction you will reduce the possibility of relapse.

Figure out which days in your week are most likely for release and work on adding something to those days, such as a haircut appointment, a meeting with a friend or family member, a sports activity, or even an online language lessons face to face.

The necessity of you going face to face with someone coupled with the knowledge of how relapsing affects one's appearance and aura should give you the motivation to avoid succumbing to a relapse for the sake of better human interactions. Your retention pays dividends to your human interactions and social life. People want to meet people with energy inside of them because that energy energises themselves, merely by association.

Every morning, write a to-do list on your smartphone or on a piece of paper.
Write the heading "To Do List". Then add bullet points and make a list of the things you will do for that day. For example:

- Reading one hour
- Exercise / run
- Writing one hour
- Study one hour
- Clean up room 15 mins

Before you start each task, set your timer to the time required. If you wrote "reading for an hour" set your timer for an hour, click "start" and begin. Try your best to accept no interruptions once the timer has started. Only pause for toilet breaks or emergencies.
Once the task is finished, tick it off. This is a very satisfying activity that brings structure and discipline to your life, two things that you are perhaps lacking and very much need in your life, in order to successfully carry out long-term semen retention.

When you start getting longer streaks you will also begin to notice changes going on in your life. In the body, in your mind, in your relationships and in your life circumstances. Especially at the beginning, you will be most sensitive to these changes taking place. For many it will be changes in the response from friends and people of the opposite sex. You may notice your eyes or features looking clearer and more alive. You may feel unusual waves of energy running through you during the day or you may even feel like punching the air when you wake up. These effects vary from person to person and for some people they don't notice anything. I recommend you start writing down your changes in a journal or in your phone notes. For example day 16 - eyes looking clearer day 24 - woman approached me. It is quite remarkable to experience these changes and it is these very changes that spur one on to commitment of the practice.

Every time you feel that a relapse is coming I want you to keep this thought in your mind. People are programmed to avoid death. For this reason they are repelled from death and thus attracted to life. Your seed represents life and the more you have of it, the more abundant life you contain thus the more people feel your essence and become attracted to it. Every time you lose your seed, your essence becomes less, and the strength of attraction people feel towards you will be ultimately less. Losing your seed means less life, less life means less attractiveness and more repulsiveness. Ask yourself the next time you are about to relapse and ejaculate, is this the entity I wish to become? A lifeless husk of the man I am today? Or do I want to be a vessel of abundant vitality, a walking entity of life energy?

Part 4 - Your Weakness (A letter from your self)

As someone who is unable to curb their own desire for pleasure, at the expense of their life and body, let me tell you this. You are as soft as they come. There is nothing special about you. And you do not deserve to own such a magnificent piece of machinery, your human body. Your body has the capabilities to change this earth. A single human body is capable of leading armies, leading nations, empowering people and ultimately improving the state of this world. You will leave this world in a better state than it was before you came into it, the world should be thankful for your existence. This is why you are here. To contribute to the betterment of humanity is what you were put here to do. Regardless of race, religion or any other lines of division, you are all here for one thing. Improvement.

Yet here you are at home, lying in your own filth, staring at pictures of porn and playing with yourself. Nothing is more important to you than your five seconds of writhing in pleasure before the floodgates of your own life force open up and drain the very essence of who you are. A traitor to your own body, sacrificing life for pleasure. Is this the level existence you will continue to live at?

Nothing about you represents being a man. Or being worthy of what you have been given. Look at yourself and ask yourself, is this the kind of man I wish to be? A slave to desire who cannot think for himself as he submits to the power of his animal instincts. Every ejaculation is a direct loss of your own powers, your vital fluids, the fluids that sparked your own life, that brought you into this existence. The universe is self-regulating, and your very act of selfishness is the very act that is withering you away into nothing, as the universe has no need for entities that act out of self-interest.

The universe helps those who help the universe.
This is a collaborative effort in which you are acting selfishly.
Your ancestors fought in wars, watched their loved ones die from starvation and disease, lived in poverty with no sanitation, and until recently, no electricity. They worked hard every day of their lives and did their all to keep their heads above water and survive. And now there you are, a soft puddle of jelly that cannot keep his hands of his own prick for long enough to do anything productive, anything worthwhile in this world.

Wake up.

It's time to do what you were brought here to do.
If you don't make this resolution now, you never will.

You are here to become stronger than 99% of men out there, draining their powers into oblivion. What you are reading now is a message from the universe. That is where I came from, as did you. You are here for a reason, you are reading this for a reason. You are here to change the world in some way. Your presence was requested to this plane of existence, and now you need to act on it and fulfill your duty as a human being. As a man. This world awaits you. You know exactly what you need to do in this universe, your mission lies within you. You need to find it, I assure you it is there. Start giving your powers to the universe and the universe will start giving powers to you. This is reciprocal, the value you provide equating to the value you become. Provide value and you become valuable. Squander resources and you become nothing. The choice is yours and you are one of the very few who came across the information to change their path for the better. How could one know this and not act on it? This is what you needed to know, and the information has found you. It is now with you to make the choice, to pull the trigger and become what it is you were brought here to be. You know what to do. The choice is yours.

Part 5 - Your Vitality

What exactly is the quality known as vitality? It is hard to pinpoint in a sentence. But you can see it in the beautiful fur coat of a jaguar, in the singing of a bird, in the scent of a rose, you can see it in the face of a healthy youth. It is the physical manifestation of abundant life in the organism. The accumulated force of life. The act of masturbation and subsequent release of semen comes at the cost of much vitality. We know that animals, plants and insects live longer when their seed is kept intact. Countless studies in biology verify the fact that reproductive action leads to deterioration of the organism and shortened lifespan.

Can you imagine the feeling of becoming more attractive? Perhaps you have felt that on certain days or during certain periods people were more drawn to you. As humans we are drawn to life and entities with an abundance of vitality. This is often reflected in aesthetic beauty, but also reflected in one's aura, in one's very being, things that have no words are conveyed through interactions that signal one's life essence and the strength of their vitality. The more of this one possesses, the more attractive they become to others around them, and not merely those of the opposite sex but those of the same sex, those of all ages, those of other species. The abundant build-up of life in a single entity becomes a magnetic force, drawing all forms of life towards it. If you provide the resources for the body to recharge itself, it will simply do just that and generate a powerful life force from within your very being.

Every day you refrain from losing fluids is another day that your body can use those fluids for the nourishment of your being. A flower that grows in nutritive soil, gets plenty of water and nourishment from the sun becomes a beautiful flower. As there are no impediments to growth, it can grow into its ideal form. When there is an insufficiency of soil, water and sunlight, the flower will suffer, and this suffering is reflected visually in the flower, as it begins to look dull and become wilted. Much the same occurs within the human. For a human to fulfill its ideal form and embody its utmost beauty it must have adequate access to the necessary elements of life. Food, water, sunlight and so on. The seed is an ultimate storehouse of energy and nutrition. The seed has a nutritive influence on the body, and the preservation of it saves the body from needlessly making more and more at the cost of overall organism integrity. Each seed loss needs to be replenished via energy from the body that all other areas of the body also require. This is what creates a deficit of resources and energy in the body that eventually comes to affect the overall appearance of the person.

Within the Indian religious traditions, "brahmacharya" is the concept of sexual chastity for the purposes of spiritual attainment. "Practice of Brahmacharya gives good health, inner strength, peace of mind and long life. It invigorates the mind and the nerves. It helps to conserve physical and mental energy. It augments memory, will force and brain power. It bestows tremendous strength, vigour and vitality. Strength and fortitude are obtained. The eye is the window of the mind. If the mind is pure and calm, the eye also is calm and steady. He who is established in Brahmacharya will have lustrous eyes, a sweet voice and a beautiful complexion." (Swami Sivananda, 1934, Ch. 8)

I want you to keep this in your mind. For every day you conserve your energies, you regenerate your body, you replenish lost sources and over time, your cells fill up with an abundant source of vitality. People around you will feel it, you yourself will feel it, the very world around you begins to change, it responds differently to your being, for your being is more in tune with nature, more in tune with the source of life. This is why you will not waste a precious drop of your life essence.

References

Practice Of Brahmacharya, Swami Sivananda, 1934, Ch. 8

Part 6 - The following is a personal account written long ago:

"A gentleman of some intelligence had lived a continent life to the age of thirty-nine. A successful manufacturer, he had acquired wealth and kept up a hospitable home, but had never married. In point of personal purity, he was regarded as a very Joseph by his friends, among whom I had the honour to enjoy a place. What was my surprise when he consulted me with reference to seminal weakness! I made careful inquiries about his habits. Had he practiced masturbation? "Never!" Had he indulged in familiarities with some woman? "Never !" And yet here was a case of frequent nocturnal emissions, with all the usual symptoms of exhaustion. (...)

I said, "There is but one explanation, and that is, that your imagination has been filled with pictures of nude women and sexual intercourse."
He owned it: "If this is important, I am free to confess that I am rarely alone a moment without being occupied with such visions. And my dreams, too, are full of them."
I explained the mischief, and warned him that unless he could break up the habit altogether, he was a ruined man.
"But," said he,"I can't prevent my thoughts, I can't decide what shall come into my mind!"
"Yes, you can," I answered; "You can decide precisely what shall occupy your mind. It is just herein that a man is superior to a horse."
"Oh," he replied, "I am sure that is impossible; the thoughts will come unbidden." (…)
" Now," said I, "You must try the following plan, and report to me. Fix it in your mind that a sensual idea is dangerous and harmful; then the instant one comes it will startle you. By an effort you change the subject immediately. You can, if you are in earnest, set such an alarm in your mind, that if a lascivious thought occurs to you when asleep, it will waken you. (A number of persons have testified to this.) If when you are awake the enemy enters your mind, you will be aroused, and expel it at once without a very serious effort. If there is a moment's doubt, spring up and engage in some active exercise of the body. Each effort will be easier, until after a week or two you will have, in this particular, complete control of your thoughts; and that will soon make you feel a good deal more like a man.
"The fever and excitement of voluptuous revery wears out the nervous system, emasculates manhood, and shuts out all the noblest visions in this and the upper world." Besides this, there must be an observance of health laws. It is idle, over-fed people who suffer most from all animal excitements. Work hard, or by brisk walking and gymnastics give yourself two or three good sweats every day, and eat plain, nourishing, unstimulating food. Go without supper. Retire early, and rise early. Drink freely of cold water both on rising and going to bed, and sleep in pure air."

Victory. After two months' faithful observance of this regimen, the patient sent me a note, which ran as follows, ''My Dear Sir: I cannot refrain from writing you of the result of your prescription. And that you may comprehend the happy change which has come over me, I will describe my condition when I sought your advice. I could not look upon a woman without my imagination being busy with her person, and when alone, I was constantly occupied with thoughts of women; and it was never with their moral qualities. Sometimes these thoughts would haunt me not only during my waking hours, but in my sleep. Three or four times a week, and sometimes every night in the week, these dreams would provoke nocturnal emissions. I must confess that during the month before I sought your advice I was in a constant fever. I loathed myself.

About a week before I consulted you, I went to New York, desperately resolved that I would seek with some abandoned woman a complete relief from my burning lust. I went so far as to order such a companion through the clerk of the hotel where I stopped, and retired to my room to await her coming. Then my mother's angel face came to me, and the sweet, loving face of that other woman—that dear girl whose untimely death has been the one great sorrow of my life, her face came and looked into mine with an unearthly love. I hurried to the office, made an excuse, hastened to another hotel, and came back to my home the next morning. All this now seems like a horrid dream.

My dear friend, I do not know in what terms to express my gratitude that all this is past. I found it difficult to control my thoughts at first, but as you advised, I soon fixed the thought of danger in my mind, so that when a lascivious fancy appeared, it startled me, and immediately I took out of my pocket the card you suggested, on which I had written ten words, each suggestive of a subject in which I am interested. Looking over this card, I had no difficulty in changing the subject at once. This policy, with daily exercise and plain food, has given me a complete victory. I can now meet my lady friends and converse with them with real pleasure. My thoughts are not more lecherous and unclean than they would be in the presence of sisters. The sense of manliness which I now feel in conversation with ladies, the real profit and social delight which their conversation affords me, these, added to cooler, better nerve, render the change a very happy one. I now believe what, you will remember, I began with doubting, namely, that the great sexual waste is in lecherous thought. And I do not see how men are to become chaste unless they can learn to control their thinking. If their brains are hot with lust, if within they throb and burn as I did, I do not see how they are to keep themselves pure without.

You will ask me about the nocturnal emissions. I can report an improvement, but I did not expect to get rid of that difficulty at once. I have no doubt, from my present condition, that I shall soon recover from this weakness and become a man again.
With grateful respect, I am your friend, G. W." (Source Unknown)

Part 7 - Stop it at the source

If you turn on a water hose and block the end with your finger then the water will build up quickly to the point where you cannot physically block the pressure and the water will come spitting out of the end. If you want to avoid the water coming out then don't just block the pressure at the end. If you really wanted to stop the water then you should never have turned it on in the first place! Likewise if you want to refrain from losing your sexual fluids then do not excite the sexual centres. By that point it is already too late. The chemical processes taking place in your body happen much before ejaculation.

The sexual thought triggers the testes into work, moving the semen up the vas deferens and ready for ejaculation. At this point, if the fluids are not ejaculated they will be excreted via the faeces and urine and perhaps some of it will be resorbed back into the body. There are perhaps benefits of this seminal resorption, but is this resorption more beneficial than the energy it took to create this valuable fluid in the first place? I think the fact that women (who don't produce semen) yet outlive men considerably might perhaps indicate that saving oneself from the creation of semen in the first place is of more benefit than that gained from semen production and resorption, at least from a longevity perspective.

Rather than stopping at the last minute, stop the thoughts from entering. Stop the process before it even starts. It is much easier to block a sexual thought before you have had any time to entertain it. Once you get worked up over the sexual thought it is a battle to keep the top from blowing off the lid.

When the thought comes to you, release it. Know that it leads to nothing good. It is a danger. When the thought hits, become aware of it, become conscious that this thought has entered your mind, like an uninvited guest. When this happens you must take physical action to rid yourself of the thought. Take a deep breath and click your fingers hard. Feel a spark of energy emanating from your heart as you click your fingers. The moment you click your fingers all remnants of the sexual thought will vanish! I was told to do this and for me, it worked. I am now telling you to do this, and for you it will also work. All you need to do is believe it. Do not underestimate the power of words. Take a deep breath, click your fingers and you will be done with that thought. It is the breaking of the spell. Trust it. The physical act of clicking your fingers will snap you out of the mind frame instantly. The sudden reverberation of sound waves will pull you into the present moment and bring you out of that mess your animal instincts have buried inside you.

See your desire as an external entity, as an invasive parasite trying to latch on to your mind, to sap your spirit. It has the addictiveness of heroin and can insidiously infiltrate your very being and drain your life force all the way down to the core, if you are not careful. Be vigilant and stop the thought before arousal begins. You're in a battle for your life

162

force. These thoughts are entities like mosquitos, that try to suck your vitality for their own survival. Do not allow that to happen! Your mind is under your own protection, it is your responsibility to protect and conserve its power.

Part 8 - Cold shower

Cold showers and cold water submersion are great ways to cool the sexual heat one feels. Whenever lust creeps up and becomes untameable, a cold shower is perhaps the best solution. Particularly making sure to put cold water over the penis and testicles for a time too to cool them off. The cold water is very purifying for the mind and body.

If you cannot stand the coldness of the water then start with a lukewarm temperature and slowly work your way down to a colder level that you are comfortable with. This practice is said to bring the blood to the surface and move it away from the built-up areas of the genital regions where stimulation has kept it concentrated. The cooling sensation quickly dampens the over-excited and stimulated state of the genitals, and the return to mental equilibrium become quickly apparent.

A full body wash under cold water has many other purported benefits too, the refreshment from the cooling of the skin and the blood, puts one into a new frame of mind and is a most effective method to rid oneself of the desirous state. Feel the benefits of a cold bath or shower, and if it works well for you use it as another weapon in your arsenal of measures against relapsing on semen retention. Of course make sure it is not a freezing day outside and do not try this if you have any health conditions or illnesses that could be exacerbated by this practice.

"All kinds of stimulating and heating substances, high-seasoned food, rich dishes, the free use of flesh, and even the excess of aliment, all, more or less — and some to a very great degree — increase the concupiscent excitability and sensibility of the genital organs, and augment their influence on the functions of organic life, and on the intellectual and moral faculties. Sexual desire, again, in turn, throws its influence over the whole domain of the nerves of organic life, as well as of the cephalo-spinal nerves, or those of animal life; particularly affecting the stomach, brain, and heart, and, to a greater or less extent, all the other organs of the body; and when it kindles into a passion, its influence is so extensive and powerful, that it disturbs and disorders all the functions of the system. Digestion is retarded, or wholly interrupted. Circulation is accelerated, and an increased quantity of blood is injected into the brain, stomach, lungs, and other important organs. Respiration is obstructed and oppressed, and imperfectly performed and insensible perspiration is considerably diminished." (Sylvester Graham, pg. 244)

Written in the 1900's:

"Many persons believe that they cannot use cold water baths; this is only because they are not accustomed to them. They will find it a comparatively easy matter to accustom themselves to the cold water in a comparatively short time, by using it at first as cool as they can bear, then a little colder each time until it can be taken entirely cold. The invigorating effects which follow will soon make it most enjoyable. Whatever the temperature, however, at which it can be taken, the daily bath should on no account be omitted." (....)

The same thing may be said of the cold air bath, which is conducive to the highest degree of health. This may be taken while going through with the exercises. Open your windows a little, at first, then a little wider each day as your body adapts itself to the temperature. The effort to keep warm will put increased vigor into the exercise and cause the blood to flow freely throughout the whole body. The writer takes his exercises nude every morning with open windows, even when the thermometer registers below zero; the colder it is, the more exhilarating and enjoyable are the exercises. It takes a little will power to jump out of a warm bed and start exercising in a cold room in winter, and when the weather is coldest there is a momentary shock, but this quickly passes away and the reaction which follows is most delightful. The pores will absorb a full supply of oxygen during this exercising which directly benefits the nervous and muscular organism; in fact, no other specific exists that will increase the virile powers of manhood like plenty of pure fresh air." (Fowler, 1913, pg. 199-200)

References

'Lectures on the science of human life', Sylvester Graham, 1839, pg. 244

'Sex Force', Fowler, 1913, pg. 199-200

Part 9 - Others sense it

The next time you feel your desires overtaking your resolve, remember these words.
Your choice to live in a world of sexual fantasy and engage in masturbatory practice does not go unnoticed by those around you.
They don't know the exact details of what you are engaging in but they sense something. Something off. Every action, word and expression will be tainted by this. This lack of vitality. Disrupted nerves. An almost palpable anxiety that a person draining their essence carries.

Many people assume their habits and true moral character to be well hidden from view and from the judgement of others. They are not.

Your very physical essence reflects exactly who you are and small cues that give clues to your inclinations and proclivities are constantly being transmitted and revealed to those around you. Women have an especially perceptive sense attuned to picking up on these cues. They experience visceral reactions from interactions with people and can pick up on subtle signs that appear as either red or green flags. Women have these evolutionary mechanisms built into them for the purposes of mate selection and self-preservation. These subtleties are often difficult to put into language as they are feelings that stem from an intuitive response based on various sensory cues.

Successful and smooth social interactions require a sensitivity of nerves and a keen sense of perceptiveness. Your brain and nervous energies are taxed heavily after semen loss.

The more optimal nutrition your body has at its disposal, the better it's ability to function; and of course this applies to all aspects of the human being; better appearance, better physical function, better mental function, more sophisticated social abilities and so on.

If you think of your own experiences, you may have perhaps even seen this yourself. A day or days after an ejaculation you seem weaker, vitality is less, response from others also weaker. Many areas are affected. This has been reported about extensively and should be easily recognised by self observation.

Try it for yourself. Maintain a good month without ejaculation, masturbation or sexually stimulating thoughts. Observe the responses you are receiving from people. Observe your social interactions. Observe how you feel talking to the opposite sex after not even thinking of the act for weeks. Things change. Increased attractiveness, confidence, and levels of energy not felt in many years begin to surface.

"Every thought has a form,
And every form is a thought expressed." (H. Butler, 1911, pg. 37)

People sense something, like an increased vitality or an abundance of life, and thus become more easily attracted to your presence. The benefits of retaining the seed have been reported by so many for so long; various religions, doctors and philosophers the world over, have attested to its value for thousands of years. Truth always stands the test of time. That such a practice has been continuing for this long, that people were reporting the benefits of restraint even before Christ, that many geniuses of note devoted their lives to it; its positive effects are undeniable.

"B. D., aged 20, had had ill health for a year or more; he was pale, feeble, nervous—lost his resolution—had no appetite—took to his bed most of the time, and became dull, almost speechless, and wholly abstracted and melancholy. His brother was his physician; but not ascertaining the cause of his symptoms, he gained no advantage over the disease, and the unhappy young man was constantly losing strength and flesh. After a while he came under the care of the writer. He was in the most miserable condition conceivable; emaciated, feeble, pallid—had night sweats, diarrhœa, or costiveness, total loathing of all food; his heart beat, his head was painful, and he felt no desire, and would make no effort, to live. Suspecting masturbation, I found, upon strict inquiry and watching, that my suspicions were well founded. I pointed out the danger of the practice, assured him that it was the cause of all his sufferings, and that he might be restored to usefulness and health again if he would strictly adhere to the course prescribed for him. He took bark and iron alternately for a long time, pursued a course of gentle exercise and invigorating diet, and gave up at once the vicious indulgence. After a long time he wholly recovered, and is now a healthy and valuable citizen." (L. Deslandes 1839, pg. 249)

References

Science discovers the physiological value of continence, R. W. Bernard, 1957,pg 1

'Practical methods to ensure success', H. Butler, 1911, pg. 37

A treatise on the diseases produced by Onanism, Léopold Deslandes 1839, pg. 249

Part 10 - Brahmacharya

The words of Swami Sivananda on Brahmachrya (The Indian concept of celibacy). "Pure air, pure water, wholesome food, physical exercise, outdoor games, walking with brisk steps, rowing, swimming, light games like tennis—all contribute to the maintenance of good health, strength and a high standard of vitality. There are indeed many ways to gain health and strength. These ways are doubtless indispensably requisite. But, Brahmacharya is the most important of all. Without Brahmacharya, all your exercises are nothing. It is the master-key for opening the realms of health and happiness. It is the corner-stone of the edifice of bliss and unalloyed felicity. It is the only specific that keeps up true manliness.

The preservation of semen is the secret of health and longevity, and of all success in the physical, mental, intellectual and spiritual planes. He who has even a little bit of Brahmacharya will tide over a crisis of any disease very easily. If it takes a month for an ordinary man for recovery, this man will be completely all right in a week.

The Shrutis declare a full life or age of one hundred years for a man. This you can attain only by the establishment of Brahmacharya. There are instances of men who have attained longevity and intellectual powers despite their loose, immoral ways. But they would have been still more powerful and brilliant had they possessed a good character and continence as well."

"After Dhanvantari had taught all the details about Ayurveda to his disciples, they enquired about the keynote of this medical science. The Master replied, "I tell you that Brahmacharya is truly a precious jewel. It is the one most effective medicine—nectar indeed— which destroys diseases, decay and death. For attaining peace, brightness, memory, knowledge, health and Self-realization, one should observe Brahmacharya, which is the highest Dharma. Brahmacharya is the highest knowledge; Brahmacharya is the greatest strength. Of the nature of Brahmacharya is verily this Atman and in Brahmacharya It resides. Saluting Brahmacharya first, the cases beyond cure, I cure. Aye, Brahmacharya can undo all the inauspicious signs."

"Practice of Brahmacharya gives good health, inner strength, peace of mind and long life. It invigorates the mind and the nerves. It helps to conserve physical and mental energy. It augments memory, will force and brain power. It bestows tremendous strength, vigour and vitality. Strength and fortitude are obtained. The eye is the window of the mind. If the mind is pure and calm, the eye also is calm and steady. He who is established in Brahmacharya will have lustrous eyes, a sweet voice and a beautiful complexion.

By the establishment of continence, vigour is obtained. The Yogi gets Siddhi or perfection by attaining perfect mental and physical Brahmacharya. Brahmacharya helps him in gaining divine knowledge and other Siddhis. When there is purity, the rays of the mind are not dissipated. Focussing of the mind becomes easy. Concentration and purity go together. Although a sage talks a few words only, a deep impression is produced in the minds of the hearers. This is due to his

Ojas Sakti, which is conserved by the preservation of semen and its transmutation.

A true Brahmachari in thought, word and deed has wonderful thought-power. He can move the world. If you develop strict celibacy, Vichara Sakti and Dharana Sakti will develop. Vichara Sakti is the power of enquiry. Dharan'a Sakti is the power of grasping and holding the Truth. If a man persistently refuses to yield to his lower nature and remains a strict celibate, the seminal energy is deflected upwards to the brain and is stored up as Ojas Sakti. Thereby the power of the intellect is intensified to a remarkable degree. The intellect becomes sharp and clear by continence. Continence increases infinitely the power of retentive memory. The strict celibate has keen and acute memory even in old age.

A man who has the power of Brahmacharya can turn out immense mental, physical and intellectual work. He has a magnetic aura around his face. He can influence people by speaking just a few words or even by his very presence. He can control anger and move the whole world. (…)Through Brahmacharya and Brahmacharya alone can you get physical, mental and spiritual advancement in life." (Swami Sivananda)

References

Practice Of Brahmacharya, Swami Sivananda, 1934, Ch. 2

Part 11 - Writings from the late 1800s and early 1900s

"The advantages arising out of the conservation of the sex force may be briefly summarised as follows:

1. The brain attains its best efficiency; men and women are therefore enabled to accomplish their best, mentally.
2. The nerves are steady and under control, showing that the health of the nervous system is perfect.
3. The organic body is at its best condition.
4. The eyes are bright and the face more attractive, even the individual features assuming more pleasing outlines. Often defective eyesight is restored.
5. There is greater contentment, thereby increasing the probability of securing happiness.
6. Increased vitality, which, with all the other advantages named, confers physical and mental power, a greater ability to enjoy life, to develop the higher nature, and attain longevity."

"Keep it firmly impressed upon your mind that a successful life is founded on the attraction of personal magnetism and this is developed from habitual self-control and the conservation of force which this insures. Do not over weary the brain or misuse the functions of the body. It will be asked by many, what is the best way of putting these teachings into practice, and how long a time is required to bring about the desired results! In answer to the first question it may be said that the first requisite is a firm determination to carry out the necessary self-denial, however hard the struggle. This means, primarily, the changing of the mental attitude, for nothing is possible that the mind regards as impossible. It means the establishment of new habits, both mental and physical, for man is a creature of habit, and many traits that are regarded as indications of character are simply evidences of habit. Many persons, habitually very active, have, after acquiring fortunes become exceedingly lazy, while lazy persons, forced by adverse

circumstances into unaccustomed activity, have developed energetic habits. Such is the force of habit, and the establishment of habits along the desired line is therefore a condition of success. As to the time required, we may answer, "none;" this means that as soon as the new method of life is taken up, the body will begin to conform. Little by little, as habits strengthen, results will appear; in small ways at first but increasing constantly as the man persists, until the desired end is attained."
(Fowler, 1913, pg. 38)

Written by John Harvey Kellog, the creator of Corn Flakes. "This is a brief sketch of the local effects of the horrid vice of self-abuse. The description has not been at all overdrawn. We have yet to consider the general effects, some of which have already been incidentally touched upon in describing nocturnal emissions, with their immediate results. General Effects: The many serious effects which follow the habit of self-abuse, in addition to those terrible local maladies already described, are the direct results of two causes in the male; viz.,

1. Nervous exhaustion;
2. Loss of the seminal fluid.

There has been much discussion as to which one of these was the cause of the effects observed in these cases. Some have attributed all the evil to one cause, and some to the other. That the loss of semen is not the only cause, nor, perhaps, the chief source of injury, is proved by the fact that most deplorable effects of the vice are seen in children before puberty, and also in females, in whom no seminal discharge nor anything analogous to it occurs. In these cases, it is the nervous shock alone which works the evil.
Again, that the seminal fluid is the most highly vitalised of all the fluids of the body, and that its rapid production is at the expense of a most exhaustive effort on the part of the vital forces, is well attested by all physiologists. It is further believed by some eminent physicians that the seminal fluid is of great use in the body for building up and replenishing certain tissues, especially those of the nerves and brain, being

absorbed after secretion. Though this view is not coincided in by all physiologists, it seems to be supported by the following facts:—

1. The composition of the nerves and that of spermatozoa is nearly identical.

2. Men from whom the testes have been removed before puberty, as in the case of eunuchs, are never fully developed as they would otherwise have been.

The nervous shock accompanying the exercise of the sexual organs—either natural or unnatural—is the most profound to which the system is subject. The whole nervous system is called into activity; and the effects are occasionally so strongly felt upon a weakened organism that death results in the very act. The subsequent exhaustion is necessarily proportionate to the excitement.

It need not be surprising, then, that the effects of the frequent operation of two such powerful influences combined should be so terrible as they are found to be.

General Debility.—Nervous exhaustion and the loss of the vivifying influence of the seminal fluid produce extreme mental and physical debility, which increases as the habit is practiced, and is continued by involuntary emissions after the habit ceases. If the patient's habits are sedentary, and if he had a delicate constitution at the start, his progress toward the grave will be fearfully rapid, especially if the habit were acquired young, as it most frequently is by such boys, they being generally precocious. Extreme emaciation, sallow or blotched skin, sunken eyes, surrounded by a dark or blue colour, general weakness, dullness, weak back, stupidity, laziness, or indisposition to activity of any kind, wandering and illy defined pains, obscure and often terrible sensations, pain in back and limbs, sleeplessness, and a train of morbid symptoms too long to mention in detail, attend these sufferers.

Consumption.—It is well recognized by the medical profession that this vice is one of the most frequent causes of consumption. At least such would seem to be the declaration of experience, and the following statistical fact adds weight to the conclusion:—

173

"Dr. Smith read a paper before a learned medical association a few years since in which he pointed out the startling fact that in one thousand cases of consumption five hundred and eighteen had suffered from some form of sexual abuse, and more than four hundred had been addicted to masturbation or suffered from nocturnal emissions."[49]

"Most of those who early become addicted to self-pollution are soon afterward the subjects, not merely of one or more of the ailments already noticed, but also of enlargements of the lymphatic and other glands, ultimately of tubercular deposits in the lungs and other viscera, or of scrofulous disease of the vertebræ or bones, or of other structures, more especially of the joints."[50]

Many young men waste away and die of symptoms resembling consumption which are solely the result of the loathsome practice of self- abuse. The real number of consumptives whose disease originates in this manner can never be known.

Dyspepsia.—Indigestion is frequently one of the first results. Nervous exhaustion is always felt by the stomach very promptly. When dyspepsia is once really established, it reacts upon the genital organs, increasing their irritability as well as that of all the rest of the nervous system. Now there is no end to the ills which may be suffered; for an impaired digestion lays the system open to the inroads of almost any and every malady.

Heart Disease.—Functional disease of the heart, indicated by excessive palpitation on the slightest exertion, is a very frequent symptom. Though it unfits the individual for labor, and causes him much suffering, he would be fortunate if he escaped with no disease of a more dangerous character.

Throat Affections.—There is no doubt that many of the affections of the throat in young men and older ones which pass under the name of "clergyman's sore throat" are the direct results of masturbation and emissions.

Dr. Acton cites several cases in proof of this, and quotes the following letter from a young clergyman:—

"When I began the practice of masturbation, at the age of sixteen, I was in the habit of exercising my voice regularly. The first part in which I felt the bad effects of that habit was in the organs of articulation. After the act, the voice wanted tone, and there was a disagreeable feeling about the throat which made speaking a source of no pleasure to me as it had been. By-and- by, it became painful to speak after the act. This arose from a feeling as if a morbid matter was being secreted in the throat, so acrid that it sent tears to the eyes when speaking, and would have taken away the breath if not swallowed. This, however, passed away in a day or two after the act. In the course of years, when involuntary emissions began to impair the constitution, this condition became permanent. The throat always feels very delicate, and there is often such irritability in it, along with this feeling of the secretion of morbid matter, as to make it impossible to speak without swallowing at every second or third word. This is felt even in conversation, and there is a great disinclination to attempt to speak at all. In many instances in which the throat has been supposed to give way from other causes, I have known this to be the real one. May it not be that the general irritation always produced by the habit referred to, shows itself also in this organ, and more fully in those who are required habitually to exercise it?"

Nervous Diseases.—There is no end to the nervous affections to which the sufferer from this vice is subject. Headaches, neuralgias, symptoms resembling hysteria, sudden alternations of heat and cold, irregular flushing of the face, and many other affections, some of the more important of which we will mention in detail, are his constant companions.

Epilepsy.—This disease has been traced to the vile habit under consideration in so many cases that it is now very certain that in many instances this is its origin. It is of frequent occurrence in those who

175

have indulged in solitary vice or any other form of sexual excess. We have seen several cases of this kind.

Failure of Special Senses.—Dimness of vision, amaurosis, spots before the eyes, with other forms of ocular weakness, are common results of this vice. The same degeneration and premature failure occur in the organs of hearing. In fact, sensibility of all the senses becomes in some measure diminished in old cases.

Spinal Irritation.—Irritation of the spinal cord, with its resultant evils, is one of the most common of the nervous affections originating in this cause. Tenderness of the spine, numerous pains in the limbs, and spasmodic twitching of the muscles, are some of its results. Paralysis, partial or complete, of the lower limbs, and even of the whole body, is not a rare occurrence. (...)

Insanity.—That solitary vice is one of the most common causes of insanity, is a fact too well established to need demonstration here. Every lunatic asylum furnishes numerous illustrations of the fact. "Authors are universally agreed, from Galen down to the present day, about the pernicious influence of this enervating indulgence, and its strong propensity to generate the very worst and most formidable kinds of insanity. It has frequently been known to occasion speedy, and even instant, insanity." (Kellogg, 1881, pg. 241-6)

References

'Sex Force', Fowler, 1913, pg. 199-200

Plain facts for old and young, J.Kellog, 1881, pg. 241-6

Part 12 - Master this practice and doors open - the path to success

Every time you decide to release, remember, you are making a choice between two worlds. It is akin to a fork in the road. A step towards preservation will bring you a step towards the sphere of life. A step towards preservation and your energy is not lost. Not only is it preserved but the surplus energy is a nutritive source of energy for all elements of your body, this in turn, charges your mind, builds your aura, and becomes your appearance. Over time, the signs of someone with vital energy become quite visual, at first appearing in the expression and over a longer period revealing the built-up vitality in your physical features.

A step in the opposite direction and the fluids are not preserved, the insufficiency must be replenished and thus will be drawn from your body. This affects all other parts that require energy as their access to it and to nutrition, becomes limited. This then has a cascade effect on many chemical functions and processes taking place from within the body. Over time the lack of energy and nutritive supply manifests itself in the body via chemical expression, movement, physical features and nervous disposition. The choices you make every day are affecting your destiny. Take responsibility for those small choices and you will be making a large scale impact on your life.

Even if you don't know where success lies at this point, the practice of conserving and building your vital forces will give you the energy you need to find out where it is you need to go. It will open up the direction of your destiny. It happened for me, it has happened for many others and if you persist it will happen for you.

Every day you refrain is a step towards a new person that already exists in another realm that is trying to get closer to you. Everyday you preserve your energy you are getting closer to your maximised potential. Your energy becomes formidable and everything in the universe will be drawn to your energy. The plants, the animals and people of all ages will sense something about you, a force of life that hits them on an energetic level. Some people see this manifest as attraction from the opposite or same sex, increased affection from previously unaffectionate people, increased interactions with strangers, increased opportunities and so on. Conversely, negative energies in your life tend to fade away.

Once your power increases, your patience for things that do not serve you gets thinner. You become a more valuable being and by merit of this fact you start to filter out things in your life that are not productive for you. The universe is organising itself to your being, this is a constant process that is always happening. The very fibre of your being plays a large role in your destiny, improve those fibres and you improve your destiny. It is nothing less than transformative. Try it for yourself. You are not sacrificing much at all when the benefits to be gained from retention are fully considered.

Part 13 - You may have heard before that semen is just protein and water..

Perhaps you feel that semen loss can be easily replenished after a good night's sleep or by drinking a glass of milk. And for that reason you feel no hesitation in releasing your built-up sexual fluids.

You may have heard that nothing of the substance of semen is of particular indispensability. I remember growing up hearing semen is just protein and water and for that reason the loss of it seemed inconsequential. However, many constituents found and studied in the semen have been shown to play vital roles in the health and maintenance of the organism. Furthermore studies in the deficiency of these constituents have reported negative health outcomes.

When you are about to give in and ejaculate, perhaps consideration of what you are actually losing may give you the motivation to curb your desirous actions. Let's have a quick look at some published works on semen analysis and see what these constituents are used for in the body. In particular we will focus on the constituents found in the semen: spermine, and it's derivative spermidine.

"When human semen 'had stood a little while, some three-sided bodies were seen in it, terminating at either end in a point; some were of the length of the smallest grain of sand, and some were a little bigger, (…) Thus, in a letter of November 1677, addressed to the Royal Society, Antoni van Leeuwenhoek reported the discovery of the crystalline substance in semen which later became known as spermine."

Within Spermine lies the constituent Spermidine. Spermidine is "a base present in the mother-liquor after separation of spermine phosphate."

"So far as spermine in human semen is concerned, there can be little doubt that its high concentration which is of the order of 50-250 mg./ lOO ml., is due chiefly to the prostatic secretion. (…) the highest values obtained by the Finnish investigator in the different organs (expressed as mg. spermine phosphate per 100 g. tissue, wet weight) were, prostate 456, pancreas 77, adrenal 58, liver 43, spleen 40, testis 29, ovary 9." (T.Mann, 1954, pg. 160).

This research was carried out in the 1950s when much was still unknown about the beneficial effects of spermidine in the body. More recent research however has shed light on this.

In a 2018 study it was asserted that spermidine delays aging in humans.
"External supply of the natural polyamine spermidine can extend life span in model organisms including yeast, nematodes, flies and mice. Recent epidemiological evidence suggests that increased uptake of

spermidine with food also reduces overall, cardiovascular and cancer-related mortality in humans." (Madeo F, et al., 2018).

"It has been suggested that spermidine may have an anti-inflammatory effect by inhibiting pro-inflammatory cytokine synthesis in human mononuclear cells (Zhang et al. 1997) and suppressing LFA-1 expression on human lymphocytes (Soda et al. 2005)."
"Spermidine can prevent memory loss in aging model organisms (Gupta et al. 2013, 2016)."
"Long-term treatment with spermidine in mice had a protective effect both on the heart and the kidney (Eisenberg et al. 2009). Senescence is associated with significant histological changes in the kidney." (Filfan M, et al., 2020).

When we consider the eye-opening benefits that spermine and spermidine have on physiological function, we must wonder how such a valuable constituent, which is found in abundance in the prostatic fluid, could be considered inconsequential to lose via ejaculation and semen loss. It appears quite logical that if such a constituent is so beneficial and has been found to extend life, then the preservation of such a constituent must be of great importance for the overall longevity of the organism. This, of course, is only my own perspective from these findings, please draw your own conclusions from looking at the data.

References

1. Madeo F, Carmona-Gutierrez D, Kepp O, Kroemer G. 'Spermidine delays aging in humans.' Aging (Albany NY). 2018 Aug 6;10(8): 2209-2211. doi: 10.18632/aging.101517. PMID: 30082504; PMCID: PMC6128428.
2. Filfan M, Olaru A, Udristoiu I, Margaritescu C, Petcu E, Hermann DM, Popa-Wagner A. 'Long-term Treatment with Spermidine Increases Health Span of Middle-aged Sprague-Dawley Male Rats.' Geroscience.

2020 Jun;42(3):937-949. doi: 10.1007/s11357-020-00173-5. Epub 2020 Apr 13. PMID: 32285289; PMCID: PMC7287009.

T.Mann, 'The biochemistry of semen', 1954, pg. 160

Part 14 - Starting Small Actions

If you are having trouble abstaining long-term then how about short-term? If I gave you a challenge, would you do it? Would you fall into the group that actually carries out the challenge, or would you skip past it? I assure you, if you are one of the few that try it, you will have more success in retaining.

The challenge is this:

Set your timer for 5 minutes, and in that time do not allow a single sexual impulse to entertain your mind. Not in the slightest. Remember, by the time the sexual thought is entertained in the mind, the blood starts heading away from the organs and down towards the genital area, the testes become activated and after a short time the sperm makes its way up the vas deferens in preparation for ejaculation. When the sexual thought comes, breathe out and let it go.
Turn on your timer for 5 minutes and do this, do this now. Go.
Did you complete it? Were you able to stop for five whole minutes without the interruption of sexual thoughts?

If you were, I think you know the next step. You are going to to do the same today or tomorrow morning. This time set your clock for an hour and in that time do not allow yourself to act on any sexual impulse you may feel. If you fail, then simply reset the timer and try again. If you can make it through an hour, you have made immense progress. These little challenges should give you a taste of what it is to go through abstinence and put you in the right mind frame. If you are feeling ready you can go ahead and set the timer for 24 hours. Start with these small steps and then you can naturally progress to longer stretches of time. Challenge yourself. Whatever excuse you have in your mind for not trying, banish it now, and realise its now or never. You have an opportunity here to become the master of your mind, not the slave. This is where YOU have to make the move. I can't help you. It's on you. You took the course, you read the words, you know what to do, NOW IT'S UP TO YOU TO DO IT. You need to move. When you finish reading these words, take action. If you can last an hour without stimulating the sexual impulse, already you are becoming very well disciplined. This is a valuable power to have. Do whatever it takes to achieve it.

Part 15 - What changes on retention?

I'll tell you what changes. The people around you. Not everybody loves everybody. We all have attractions and aversions to others, this is a natural process. Just as an engine has its own unique individual parts that only connect to other certain parts in order to make the engine run, so too do humans connect to the humans that are most suitable.

We should not expect to go about connecting with everyone, we should have an understanding that we were created to connect with certain people and not with others. Knowing this we must know that it is the person we are, it is our life essence that determines the unspoken visceral feelings that others will feel towards us; and furthermore the essence of who we are determines what we are and are not drawn too. Retaining your seed increases your essence dramatically overtime, especially for one that has spent many years wasting their life essence on sensual gratification. This essence you are building is not only affecting yourself, it is affecting the world around you, and how the people of this world respond to you.

Many of the connections you have made may not stand the transformation you are undergoing whilst retaining. It is like you are becoming a whole new human being, and in a sense you are. You have sealed the leaks that were draining your resources and are now slowly regenerating the energy of your life force. You are becoming an attractive force in the world. One that others will be drawn to, one that will stir the emotions of those you interact with and leave a lasting impression.

You are carrying god's energy within you, and you are carrying more of it than you have ever had, more of it than perhaps most others have. How can you not make an impression on others? It's inevitable. With this in mind, realise how valuable your essence is when kept within your body, to nourish your brain, nourish your blood, to nourish all your organs, vitalise your energy, raise your spirit and increase the energetic aura of life that is within you. Many of the people that attracted you during your lust-filled years may no longer be so appealing to you on retention. As your moral fibre becomes stronger, the less-than-moral acquaintances in your life may not feel the same affinity to you as they once did. Allow this to happen.

If you are taking steps to conserve your life essence then you can trust that the universe is arranging your life in the appropriate way. This universe is a system of arrangements, much like the engine. Embrace the changes taking place and trust that if anybody is drifting away from you during this transitional period, that it was supposed to happen this way, and it is in your very best interests to allow it to happen. Allowing the natural flow of things will yield you the best results.

Moving into a higher frequency of energy will attract other higher frequencies of energy towards you, and at the same time drive away some of the lower and perhaps more dangerous frequencies. There are transformative processes taking place when retaining, taking place on both micro and macro levels, these changes are profound and the noticeable differences will differ from person to person. Have faith in this process, you know what you are doing, your inner compass has never been stronger as your conserved forces are building your inner intuitive faculties of premonition and telepathy, via the strengthening of your mind and glands. It will take time to regenerate but you will see so much progress on the way that you'll never lose the motivation to keep going. Every time you come close to losing your vital energy, remember these words and remember that what you are holding onto is not worth losing, it is your very life force that you are keeping inside you.

Part 16

The first and perhaps most often reported benefit of Semen Retention is increased energy. The feeling of lust, is an energy that men carry. Engaging the reproductive organs in the production and ejaculation of semen is a biological process requires much energy from the body's reserves.

That a great deal of energy is lost after ejaculation should be known to any man who has engages in sex or masturbation. Energy is the fuel for life. It is said that the restraint of the sexual energies provides more energy for every other function taking place within the body. Masturbation for men in most cases results in the ejaculation of semen from the reproductive tract. It can be thus classified as a reproductive activity. We know that reproductive activities require much energy and in many plants and animals, the use of these energies negatively affect the overall lifespan of the organism.

To keep the energy within you and not release it, will give you a powerful buzz throughout the day. You will feel as if a ball of energy resides within, electrifying your senses, and vitalising your energy stores. During long periods of retention many experience intense energy in all fields of life. Communication with others suddenly becomes more engaging, the taste of food gets better, the sense of sight, smell and hearing may become more acute. The eyes become very sharp and clear. The mind becomes lighter, and many of those who previously suffered from brain fog or mental disturbance, may find themselves feeling much more clear-headed and lighter in thought.

To stop depriving yourself of energy, to put a stop to the leaks of vitality, it is no surprise that such benefits are so commonly voiced for those practicing retention. You become a growing ball of energy. The electric charge inside of your body becomes strong, your spark becomes brighter and your life essence increases. With this knowledge how could one ever consider losing such a vital fluid for a few seconds of sense pleasure. For those retaining, you are building yourself into a new form, experiencing a new mode of living, away from the animal instincts and towards a higher plane of living, towards replenishment of the mind. This puts you in connection with creative thought.

"The only true creative function is that of . . . the faculty of formative thought ." Creative power is that which consciously makes the subjective objective, by exercise of intensely concentrated thought. It goes far beyond what is so often considered to be the creative power of artists, who even at their best are but extremely skilful artisans giving more or less perfect physical form to what they observe in visible objects, or to what in moments of inspiration may have been impressed on them. 1 * The real power of creation rests in the mind. And it can manifest only after the mind has been freed from any connection with sex, and has become indissolubly linked with spirit." ('The Coiled Serpent', Van Vliet, 1939, pg. 34).

Part 17 - The road to degeneracy

People tend to degenerate when they are spending a lot of time alone, without working towards any aim or purpose in life. Spending long stretches of time alone causes one to get caught up in unhealthy habits and addictions without the pressure of anyone else to think about. Drinking too much alcohol, watching too much TV, staying up many hours past sundown or worst of all, the excessive practice of the solitary vice, masturbation.

All such acts accelerate aging, and degenerate one physically and mentally. Accompanied by this degradation comes the eventual degradation of one's thoughts and morals, assuming they were present to begin with. A sense of apathy may develop in one living in constant solitude without a purpose or aim. Of course some people may prefer solitude, or living alone, and that can work beneficially for some, but there need to be some social commitments, some daily interactions with other humans to keep the mind from becoming apathetic to others. If one is living alone and struggling with semen retention then a particularly powerful, yet perhaps unpopular cure, is to change your living arrangements!

To cohabitate with your partner, to live with family members, to share with a friend or even to enter a share-house. Such situations should deter or at the very least significantly decrease the frequency of degenerate practices such as the solitary vice.

Of course marriage in particular carries the risk of sexual excess in those couples that do not adhere to nature's laws, yet with the knowledge of the evils of excess one can navigate this dynamic with careful discipline by not over expending themselves or their partner. It is a simple fact that the presence of other humans creates a social environment, which changes our behaviors and thoughts towards more social forms of expression, and diverts much attention away from purely self-satisfying pursuits, such as masturbation. Such is the case for animals in the wild versus those in captivity. Masturbatory activity is overwhelmingly more frequent in animals in captivity compared to those in the wild. In old medical literature, this excess activity of the solitary vice was often attributed as a cause of mental degeneration and insanity in people.

Part 18 - A personal account

These are things I have noticed after many years of practicing semen retention.

A sharper mind. I can absorb more details from conversations with people. I often remember small details of information from conversations with people and on occasion they have been surprised when I bring up those details again.

I can find the next logical step in an idea or conversation so that I can carry the conversation to the next logical point comfortably. Previously, I would often get stuck mid-conversation and lose my train of thought. I feel that my brain unconsciously now flows at a natural pace and is more than able to easily keep up with where the conversation is going.

My hearing is clearer. I can hear bells and ambient sounds from outside that my partner doesn't hear. I can hear very small sounds at night time, which often get me out of bed. It is perhaps a blessing and a curse, but the increased sensitivity to sounds and volume seems apparent.

More people interact with me. I get more messages, more invitations, have had more luck with women, and seem to be just more popular in general compared to when I wasn't retaining.

I am having more success in work.

I look healthier in the face particularly. If I compare myself to photos from many years before, I actually look younger now than in my older photos from 12 years before. Some close friends have also commented on this.

I can sleep more easily and at an earlier time.

I don't smell bad. Even if I don't shower for a while I never get terribly bad body odour. I recall this not being the case in my 20's before starting. I am not entirely sure if it is related but I sense it is somehow connected.

My mind is, for the most part, calmer and more controlled.

Sometimes when I am walking I get a feeling of immense energy that I find hard to contain, it is a very positive feeling - a sense of excitement that is close to giddiness. It's the kind of energy that makes me want to run all the way home. This is in stark contrast to my mid 20's where I was most often feeling drained, lethargic and sleepy.

This was the first area in life I became quite disciplined in, and from then on I was able to become more disciplined in other areas such as diet, movement, sleep, hygiene and so on. I feel that practicing a continent life allowed me to bring that strength into other areas that required it.

Many of the benefits are perhaps less easily defined with language because they are a meld of many things coming together. It feels that as things in various aspects improve, I fall into an improved state of flow, or existence; the world itself seems to respond more favourably to me being here, and for that I am most appreciative, most satisfied and most grateful for having found this valuable practice.

Made in the USA
Monee, IL
13 November 2024

70068150R00105